MIND

GOING
to
BAT

Published by Knights Of
Knights Of Ltd, Registered Offices:
119 Marylebone Road, London, NW1 5PU

www.knightsof.media
First published 2024
001

Written by Sunita Chawdhary
Text copyright © Sunita Chawdhary, 2024
Cover and inside art copyright © Sunita Chawdhary, 2024
All rights reserved
The moral right of the author and illustrator has been asserted

Set in Bembo Std / 15.5 pt
Typeset design by Sophie McDonnell
Typeset by Sophie McDonnell
Printed and bound in the UK

All rights reserved. No part of this publication may be reproduced or transmitted in any form or by any means, electronic or mechanical, including photocopying, recording, or any information storage or retrieval system, without prior permission in writing from the publishers. If you are reading this, thank you for buying our book.

A CIP catalogue record for this book will be available from the British Library

ISBN: 9781913311698

MIND and ME
GOING to BAT

SUNITA CHAWDHARY

KNIGHTS OF

CHAPTER 1

'How do you say 'Dear'?'

I pushed my pen into the paper and watched the ink spread a little.

'*Pree-yuh,*' Mama replied in Hindi, rolling out a *chapatti* on the stone worktop.

I knew Mama wouldn't look up now. She was too busy. I didn't look up either. *I* was busy too.

Dear Grandpa ...

P-r-ee-y-uh ...

G-r-an-d-p-a ...

Mind spelled out the sounds of the letters in Hindi, as we made a start on the letter I'd meant to write almost a year ago.

How did we know it had been a whole year since I last wrote to Grandpa?

Well, it was just before Tanya and Anya's 7th birthday party when we last wrote to him. And now there were only two weeks to go 'til they turned 8 ...

TWO WEEKS TO PARTAYYY TIME!!

Mind pointed with a shimmy towards the bowling alley invitation card we'd pinned up on the wall calendar. It was printed on shiny photo paper and I'd put it right in the middle of the month of April. So there was no way we could miss it.

Then I looked back down at the letter Grandpa had sent me in reply to mine. The paper was crumpled and torn. I hadn't bothered to keep the letter safely in my memory box of special things from Grandpa, so it had gotten lost and took ages to find.

Mind tried to press the creases out . . . *How could we let it get ruined?!*

We'd left it so long to write back, that Mind couldn't remember what Grandpa had written in his last letter to us, without looking at it again.

At least we found it in the end . . . Pfffffffft! Mind blew at it, still trying but failing to straighten the paper out.

Grandpa's handwriting looked weaker and wobblier than I remembered. Then Mind noticed he had scribbled the date in the top right corner.

It's almost as if he forgot to leave enough room and then couldn't quite fit it in.

I tried to think of what I could write about to Grandpa. Grandpa wasn't like anybody else I knew. He liked to do things his own way. He always said that *following* was for lemmings. Just because everyone else likes to use phones now, and spend all their time looking at screens for just about *everything,* he wasn't about to change his mind and follow the herd. His mind was set on going the *other* way ... So he refused to buy a phone! He said that the only real connection you make when you use a screen is plugging the charger in. He said there was something special about connecting with each other when you write a letter: it feels like you're sending a bit of yourself to someone you love, who then sends back to you a bit of them to take with you wherever you go and keep with you forever.

When I first started writing letters to Grandpa, it was just a fun way to practice my Hindi with Mama! It was a part of me, she would say, and important to hold on to. I loved filling Grandpa in on everything going on here and hearing about him in our letters. We usually couldn't wait for his replies in the post, Mind and me! Opening the envelope from India when Grandpa sent us a letter felt like we had another missing piece of a precious puzzle; one made up of our memories of Grandpa and our home in India. And Grandpa always said that reading my letters made him feel like he was right here with us.

He couldn't travel much anymore, so we hadn't seen Grandpa since we left India. It was strange. Someone who we once saw every day, we didn't see at all any more. And we had no idea when we would see him again.

I felt more than a bit guilty that I hadn't written back to Grandpa for such a long time. But Mind had a different take on it that spurred me on –

Grandpa will be just as happy to see a letter from us now as he would have been a year ago. PLUS, we have so much more to tell him, like all of the exciting things we've been up to over the past year! Like finding Pooey after she went missing . . .

Mind was right. What an adventure we'd been on! Ever since we'd gotten my pet rabbit Pooey, Grandpa loved to hear about her. Whenever we sent him updates we called it *Khargoshi Khabari!* That meant: Rabbity News! But believe it or not, I hadn't got round to telling him about the time Pooey got LOST and how we finally found her using everything *he* had taught us about ... playing CRICKET!

Go for it! Mind nudged the nib of my pen. *That's a GREAT way to start!*

Then again, I really wanted to tell Grandpa about everything that was happening right now. It was back to school tomorrow after the holidays – the start of a brand new term *and* a brand new club ... CRICKET CLUB! It was all *my* idea.

AHEM! (Oh, and Mind helped with the idea too.)

There was so much going on . . . Where to begin?!

My gaze drifted back over to the pink glittery party invitation. Clearly Tanya had won on the choice of colour this year. Being twins meant that Tanya and Anya shared their birthday. They have a big party at the bowling alley every single year. Anya would *never* have gone for something so bright and sparkly.

Mind imagined the twins tussling over their invitations, making me smile.

Having my cousins Tanya and Anya living so nearby is the best thing about being here. It means that the three of us go to the same school and we get to play together every weekend – usually at our place because Aunty Dolly likes to come over for a 'change of scene', as she puts it. But, over the half-term holiday, Tanya and Anya were away visiting their Dad. I had really missed them.

Wonder if they missed us too? Mind was never sure if Tanya and Anya thought about us anywhere near as much as we thought about them. After all, they had each other.

Mind you, we've hardly thought about Grandpa lately . . . Mind realised.

It had been a BUSY time. Since we left India and moved here, years ago, I missed

Grandpa less and less with each year. I couldn't remember much about India at all. I was only three years old when we left!

Mind turned into a magician and tried to conjure up a memory of India. A sight or sound, a smell or taste, anything would do, but we had ...

NOTHING.

I stared out of the window, my face as blank as the piece of paper I was supposed to be writing on. It was another rainy day and the back garden looked just like it did on the day we saved Pooey. Mind wanted to feel that winning feeling again.

Mind picked an apple from the fruit bowl on the kitchen table, ready to replay the brilliant ball we'd bowled, that had helped us save the day all those months ago. Mind tossed the apple up with a flick of a wrist before catching it.

How's that? Mind's eyebrows hopped up and down, with a cheeky grin underneath.

'You mean, HOWZAT!' I remembered the way bowlers *actually* said it to the umpire (that's the person on the cricket field who makes all the big decisions, like deciding if the batter is bowled out or not).

Then, Mind swooped past, like the fastest fast-bowler you've ever seen, both arms stretching out wide and cutting through the air, like the blades of a windmill going around in giant circles. Without actually chucking the hard apple (*Mama says no throwing indoors!* Mind squeaked), Mind pretended to bowl it and yelled out, pointing at me as if *I* was the Umpire:

Mind imagined bowling someone out and everyone in the crowd cheering for us to win, as I, the umpire, in charge of *everything*, lifted a finger to the sky to signal: OUT!

Yes! Let's GO OUT!!! Mind pulled at my dungaree straps, desperate to go find our old cricket set and play.

Right on cue, sunshine splashed in through the backdoor, lighting up the laundry room and our exit. It had stopped raining! But, who had opened the backdoor?

I looked at Mama. She was still busy making *chapattis*. She was concentrating so hard on dusting the rolling pin with flour, she probably wouldn't have noticed even if we *did* throw an apple across the kitchen.

Mind knew better than to risk it. The last time we threw something inside the house (my space-hopper) Pooey had gotten such a fright, she'd hopped so high that she nearly ended up hopping herself into space!

Lesson learned! Mind put the apple down.

But, I still needed to finish my letter to Grandpa.

You've made a start and we need a break, so let's go . . . Mind moaned at me. *It's already a year late, so one more day isn't going to matter!*

Mind was changing like the weather. As tempting as it was to go out and play, I had to keep us on track. I twisted the pen lid off, ready to write.

TAP . . . TAP . . . TAP!

Where's that coming from?

Mind ran over to the back door and the sound got louder — a light tapping at first, followed by a solid **KNOCK . . . KNOCK . . . KNOCK!**

But, it wasn't the knock of someone knocking at the door, or the knocking of Mama's car when she turns the key to get the engine going and it just won't start up ...

It sounded to Mind and me, like ... *THE KNOCKING OF A CRICKET BAT?!*

That got us wondering ... WHERE ON EARTH was Grandpa's lucky cricket bat, the one he gave us just before we left India? It was SO special to him and to us.

Like our letters, it was another piece of the puzzle of memories that Mind usually kept safely tucked away, for us to pull out whenever we needed it. Grandpa gave us his lucky bat to take along on our journey, in the hope that wherever we went, even when we couldn't go together, part of him would be with us that we could always remember him by. We had *promised* to keep it safe forever.

But what if, just like his last letter, we've LOST it?!

IMAGINE if we could find his bat and send him a photo of us playing cricket with it? He would LOVE that. It would make him smile such a big smile that there wouldn't be any room left on his face for any kind of sad feeling. He would know that we were always thinking of him, even when we were apart. And that he mattered enough to us that we looked after the things he gave us, like his lucky bat.

Mind was sure that the bat was the KEY that would UNLOCK all the *magical* memories stored somewhere deep inside us; of India and of our time growing up with Grandpa. Just holding it again would take us back there, to the first time Grandpa taught us how to hold a cricket bat.

I bet it still smells of Grandpa!

We breathed in and stepped forward, imaginary bat in hand, like we were taking guard, marking where we would stand on the pitch, ready to hit a SIXER! *That* is when you hit the ball so HARD and so HIGH that it shoots like a star through the sky over the boundary of the playing field and right OUT OF SIGHT! Now, *that* was a shot worth wishing for.

We *had* to go outside now.

Letter – later! Fun – first! Mind grabbed my arm and we lunged forwards.

Jumping out into the bright sunny garden, we were like a pair of skydivers ready to freefall!

CHAPTER 2

THUD.

We landed with both feet, firm and flat against the stony slabs of the patio. So much for a thrilling freefall!

Looking around, we couldn't SEE anything that was knocking. Worms were wriggling out from underground because of the rain. Birds were tweeting tunes in the trees. But there was no sign of anyone *knocking* anything.

KNOCK . . . KNOCK . . . KNOCK!

We heard it again! The sound scared Mind, who had turned into a squirrel and raced around a tree trunk all the way up to its top branches.

KNOCK! KNOCK!

It was coming from BEHIND us! Squirrel-Mind chased me around the side of the house where our garden gate had been left open, like a clue perfectly placed and pointing to where we needed to look next.

It was chilly in the shadows. Wet gravel scrunched under our feet and we became explorers trekking through snow covered terrain in climbing boots. At the end of the path (or *at the top of the mountain* – according to Mind!) we found one very

serious-looking Papa, leaning over in a batting stance, wearing thick gloves and holding the long handle of a . . . SPADE!

Not a cricket bat, after all . . . Mind was disappointed.

Papa squatted down and pressed the soil gently with a gloved hand. Then, hunching over, he knocked the muddy spade into the wooden sides of his vegetable patch, setting them deeper into the ground.

KNOCK! KNOCK! KNOCK!

'Maya! Want to help me plant these?' He grinned and waved a couple of packets of seeds at us.

He chucked a pack our way and I caught it with both hands, pulling my hands backwards like a fielder catching a fast-paced cricket ball.

Nice catch! Mind nodded proudly.

I knelt down on one knee, excited to do something together with Papa. He had worked long days this week, which meant he left early in the morning before I was up and some nights he got home so late that it was past my bedtime and I didn't get to see him at all. But it was the weekend at last. And the weekend was *our* time . . .

Time for fun and . . . GAMES!!! Mind poked me with an elbow, reminding me that we were here to play the one and only *game* of cricket.

'Papa, do you know where my lucky cricket bat is . . . the one Grandpa gave me?' I jumped up, my eyes wide now. Papa was bound to know where it was. We'd find it super quick with Papa's help. We were only moments away from feeling like we were back in India with Grandpa.

'Nope! *Nahin! NICHT!'* Papa didn't even

look up at me as he skipped through every language he knows (English, Hindi and German) just to say 3 NOs!

Mind wasn't paying attention anymore either, too distracted by shaking packets of seeds next to my ear, like maracas, making the most *annoying* rattling sound.

NO ONE cared.

My neck felt hot. The feeling crept up and

across my whole face. Like warm mountain springs, tears streamed down my cheeks.

Papa stopped and stared at me.

'What happened?!'

Me bursting out crying all of a sudden had shocked him. And Mind couldn't think straight, seeing me wobble!

I couldn't tell Papa what happened because I didn't even know myself!

He took his muddy gloves off and put one of his heavy, hairy arms around my shoulders.

'Hmm . . . I know what might cheer you up . . .' He tore open a packet and poured the tiny seeds out, from the palm of his hand into mine. The skin on his hand was dry, with lines of mud in the cracks, almost like he had drawn them on.

'Do you know what these are?' He rubbed the seeds with a finger, like he was drawing a small circle in sand.

They were small and grey, almost like the sunflower seeds that Mama likes to garnish her salad with.

Ooooohhh . . . MAGIC seeds?! Mind had a closer look and a guess.

'*These*, Maya, are *carrot* seeds!'

CARROTS?! Mind wasn't impressed. Unlike Pooey, whose ears always pricked up at the mention of her favourite veggie, Mind had almost lost all interest in what Papa was saying.

But, then Papa whispered and Mind instantly turned back to listen in. Funny how the harder it is to hear something, the more we want to hear it!

'Not just *any* carrot seeds . . . *These* are the seeds that will grow into the *crunch-iest* and CARROT-IEST carrots you've EVER seen. There will be no carrot-ier carrot out there!' Papa sighed and looked out into the distance, as though he was someplace else.

Mind wondered what Papa meant. How carroty could carrots get?

A carrot's a carrot, after all . . .

'Not even Mr Rao's carrots, winner of the Greenest Garden Competition yet *again* last year, are going to be as carroty as these.'

Then, Papa leaned in so close that his lips almost touched the little pile of seeds in my hand, as if he was about to blow them to make a wish, and he said wistfully:

'All the carrots of all the tomorrows, are in the seeds of today . . .'

He took a pinch of seeds from me, sprinkled them like seasoning over the ground and patted the soil. Then he tickled the top of my head before placing his hand on it, as if he was trying to plant a seed there too.

'Do you remember, so many flowers grew here last year?' He smiled.

Mind remembered last summer when the patch of soil where Papa had planted seeds was covered in delicate flowers. In fact, Papa had said at the time, he'd got more flowers than fruit! He couldn't even enter the Greenest Garden Competition last year and Mr Rao's carrots won again, as usual.

But instead of getting upset about it, Papa had pointed at the flowers and recited our mantra: *'Vielen Dank, für die Blumen!'*

That means: 'Thank you for the flowers'. No matter what happened, we could always be happy about the flowers.

'Maya!' Mama popped her head out of the window in the wall next to us and made Mind jump, almost making me spill the seeds everywhere. 'Why have you got all that dirt in your hand?!'

'Careful – that's not dirt,' he corrected her. '*Those*, right there, are going to be my prize-winning carrots!'

'Well my prize-winning *chapattis* are waiting for you both to come inside and eat them,' Mama wasn't joking. She *hated* when we let food get cold.

Papa tapped Mama on the top of her head playfully and came out with a rhyme, just like his big sister Aunty Dolly would:

> *'The mind is like a garden,*
> *Thoughts are like seeds,*
> *You can grow carrots,*
> *Or you can grow weeds!'*

Then, Papa's forehead wrinkled into a determined frown. 'I've *got* to do better than last year.'

Mama rolled her eyes and sighed, 'You *mean*, better than the Rao's.'

'More like, the *Wows* . . .' Papa muttered to himself as he crouched down again, rubbing the soil with a worried look.

Mr Rao *always* wins. And he isn't the only one. Sara Rao (that's his daughter) is in my class, and wins at least one gold medal every year at our school's Sports Day. I wouldn't mind so much if she wasn't such a SHOW-OFF. If *I* ever won a medal at Sports Day, I would wear it and put it on show, for sure. But I wouldn't go on and *on* and ON about it! Would I . . . ?

Brace yourself for more of Sportsday Superstar Sara's showing-off at school tomorrow . . . I hadn't realised Mind was still holding on to that worry.

'You'd better watch out for the green-eyed monster!' Mama shook her head at Papa.

MONSTER?!

Mind was confused. Papa spotted my face full of fear.

'Don't worry, Maya . . . there are *no* monsters. It's just a way of saying someone feels jealous. Mama thinks that *I* am jealous of Mr Rao. I think *Mama* is jealous of my prize carrots!' he joked.

'Don't be too long!' Mama disappeared back inside the house, her words hanging in the air like the smell of hot *chapattis* wafting out of the window she'd left open.

Papa showed me how to scatter the seeds. Letting go of the seeds I had been holding onto gave Mind a FREE feeling.

We'd done our bit and it was out of our hands now. It was like planting morsels of hope. Hope for new life, new beginnings and maybe even some winnings!

CHAPTER 3

'*Chal chapatti chakna!* Let's go chew chapattis!' Papa stroked his belly and then prodded mine with the gloves he had taken off, directing us to the back door like a farmer herding sheep.

But what about the CRICKET BAA-T?! Mind bleated, tugging at me to stay outside.

'You know what, Maya? I reckon it might be in the garden shed!' Papa winked at me.

I looked at him in wonder – how did he know what was on my Mind?!

'I'm sure that's where Grandpa's cricket bat is,' he smiled to himself.

So Papa *was* paying attention to me after all, and he *did* care! I was too excited to say *thank you,* so I just hugged his arm as tightly as I possibly could.

'Right *after* food!' Papa marched inside the house, leaving his garden gloves and wellies on the patio and the spade leaning against the wall. 'We'll put all this gardening equipment back in the shed *later* too.' Papa couldn't read my Mind, as it turned out. AFTER and LATER were *not* words we wanted to hear right now.

Mind sighed . . . *Grown ups have SO many ways of saying NO!*

I felt differently about it. It wasn't exactly a NO from Papa but it wasn't

NOW either, which was what we needed.

Then, all of a sudden, the thought struck me – like a cricket ball striking the bails off the stumps of the wicket when someone's bowled a winner! We were STUMPED.

That's exactly what we will be at Cricket Club tomorrow if we don't have a bat to hit the ball with and keep our wicket safe! Mind teased.

GURRRGGLE, my tummy purred.

It was already lunchtime. The afternoon would soon be over and *that* meant bedtime was only a few hours away. We wouldn't have any time tomorrow morning *before* school to look for our cricket stuff and then it was Cricket Club straight *after* school! We couldn't turn up to a *cricket* club without any *cricket* stuff – we would look ridiculous!

A bit like the time we turned up at WRITING Club with nothing to WRITE with! Mind shuddered at the memory of that messy moment.

Only, this was worse because *we* were the ones starting this club. There was no reason whatsoever for not being prepared.

We had to go look for that cricket bat ourselves. It was NOW or NEVER.

I rolled Mind up into a *chapatti* telescope and looked through one end, towards the garden shed.

Papa said he'd got the gardening equipment out of the shed and we knew he hadn't put it back yet . . . so he *must* have left the shed open!

We couldn't wait any longer. Our precious memories of Grandpa and our old home in India (*and* us having any chance of batting at Cricket Club) ALL depended on finding that bat!

Checking that no one was watching us from the kitchen window, Mind raced me to the shed. When we got there, we had to pull aside the leaves from the overgrown bushes like curtains and then pushed our way through the wild grass that was so tall it looked like it had *never* been mowed. It was out of reach and rarely visited by Mind and me; we couldn't remember the last time we had been to the shed.

Finally, we got to the little path of wonky concrete that led to the door, and made our way over it like we were hopping along stepping stones. There were thorny leaves and stinging nettles everywhere.

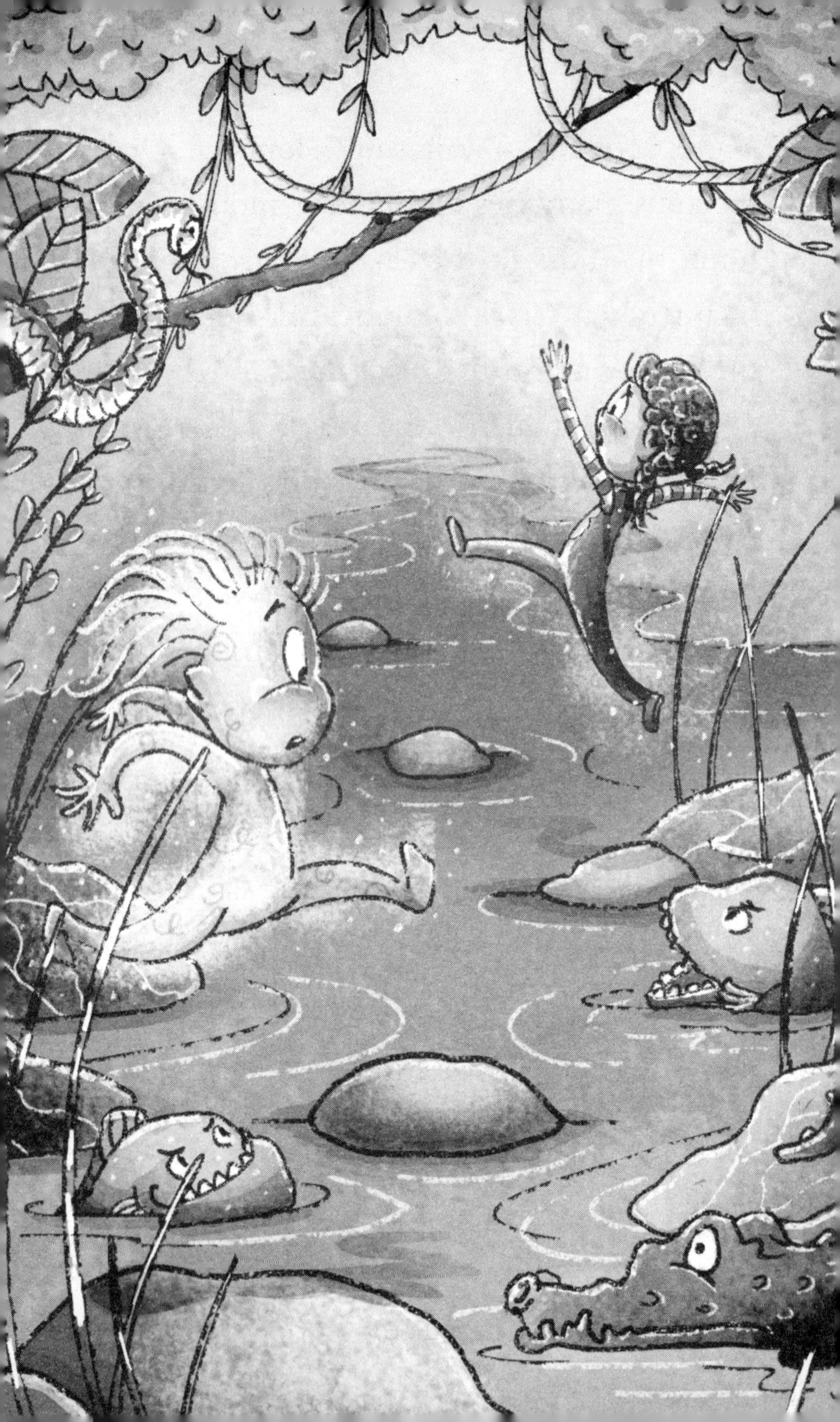

Mind pictured us crossing a river full of crocodiles and piranhas.

One wrong foot and that's the end of that!

Just as we thought, the latch of the shed had been left undone and sure enough, the door was open. It looked dark and dingy inside, through the slight gap between the door and its frame. The metal latch was rusty and the wooden panels of the shed were damp and rotting. Before pulling the door wider open, I stopped to look around. It felt like someone was following us. But, there was just a sparrow hopping around in the twigs under our feet.

Mind heard something else that made us stop again: **GRRRRHHHH . . .**

But, it was just another funny sound from my hungry belly.

We crept inside, leaving the door slightly open to let some light in. Our eyes scanned the floor, over and over again. There was STUFF everywhere! It was such a small space, and so full that it felt like we would NEVER find anything in there. Everything was covered in a thick layer of dust. I stepped in and twisted my body away from a creepy cobweb in the doorway, while Mind inspected it closely for any spiders.

I wasn't so sure it was a good idea to come here by ourselves.

BANG! The door swung shut behind us.

My heart thumped just as hard against my chest, until Mind reminded me why we were here in the first place.

We've got to find that bat for Grandpa and for tomorrow!

We'd be back inside the house in no time, tucking into some lunch and then packing our bags ready for our first day back at school. I couldn't wait to see Tanya and Anya. I wondered if they would join the Cricket Club too.

Tanya wouldn't be able to resist the chance to win at something! Aunty Dolly tells us that from the moment she had the twins, Tanya always wanted to be first at everything – she was even BORN first (a few minutes before Anya). Anya would definitely back me, so I was sure she would join my club, even if no one else did. Now, we just needed to find that cricket bat . . .

If I was a cricket bat, where would I be . . . ? Mind imagined.

'Aha!' I spotted a tall cardboard box . . . as tall as cricket-bat-Mind!

It was standing upright next to the only window in the shed. The glass pane was cracked and covered in green moss on the outside, so it wasn't much of a window for looking through anymore. But it let in just enough light to lead us to this box.

It looked just like one of the boxes that Mama and Papa had packed all our things in when we moved here. The tape sealing the box had peeled away and so it was easy to lift the flaps open. It was filled with what looked like folders and old photo albums. One of them had such a pretty cover; it looked like a beautiful *saree* design. I flicked it open to find photographs of Mama and Papa from when they got married – it was their wedding album!

I took it out of the box to show them and something fell out of it. A very old photo, so faded it almost looked black and white, had come loose and lay between my feet. I picked it up and squinted my eyes at the blurry picture of a girl with a cricket bat. Mind tilted my head to one side, as we tried to figure out the photo.

WHO?

WHAT?

WHERE?

WHEN?

STOMP! STOMP! STOMP!! STOMP!!!

Uh oh! Someone's coming! Mind slid the photo into my pocket.

I was sure it was Mama, cross that I hadn't listened to her and that my lunch was getting cold. What were we going to tell her?!

NO LIES! Mind warned me, wide eyed. It hadn't gone very well for us the last time we told lies. That wasn't the answer.

STOMP! STOMP! STOMP!

The footsteps were getting closer and faster, but they didn't sound like Mama's. *Who* was it? Just as we were about to stick the big wedding album back in its box, the door creaked open –

'Maya!' Papa appeared, out of breath and with one hand on his chest, like it was the biggest surprise ever to see me.

Phew! Only Papa! But Mind's relief

soon turned into regret!

'Thank goodness you're here!' Papa sighed loudly, leaning forward with both hands resting on his knees as he breathed hard.

'Maya *milli, kya*?!' Mama came bouncing in behind him, sounding just as panicked, asking Papa if he'd found me. She often spoke in Hindi when things got STRESSY.

Mama launched herself at me and held on to me like she would never let go again.

'We had no idea where you were!' Papa sounded cross.

I felt awful. All this while I was just thinking about Mind and me, about how we were feeling and wanting to play cricket, not sparing a thought for poor Papa and Mama as we snuck away without telling anyone.

'Sorry . . .' I said quietly, looking down at my feet. It felt like they were two heavy bricks, stuck to the ground with cement.

Mind was in shock. It wasn't like Papa to lose his cool.

'It's okay, as long as you're safe. Please don't *ever* go off on your own again without telling us.'

'What were you doing out *here*, anyway?' Mama finally took her eyes off me and looked around the shed.

'Ah, I think *I* know what Maya was up to!' Papa put his hand up, like he was a student in class answering the teacher's question. 'Maya's been trying to find Grandpa's cricket bat!'

'It's in this box here!' I reached into the same box I'd been exploring before Mama and Papa got here.

But, all I found inside it was a string

of fairy lights. It was a tangled mess. The lights weren't even on, so it was just a dull-looking, long, and wiry thing.

Mind was *extremely* disappointed, slumping to the floor. It was like Mind had given up. I'd really believed Grandpa's bat was going to be in there. It was the most important thing he'd given us to remember him by. We'd never find it now!

My eyes filled with tears that spilled over and splashed onto the ground.

'What's the matter?' Mama knelt down to give me a cuddle.

'I can't find Grandpa's bat anywhere . . . It's one of the things he gave us when we left India. If we lose it, we'll lose our memories of him.'

'Aw, Maya, I can understand why you might think that. But memories don't always have to come from *things*. You can remember someone in all sorts of ways. It can be a *sound*, a *smell*, a *taste*, a *touch* . . . Sometimes it's something you *see*, or something you *can't* see, like a *feeling* that reminds you of them. Often, it's something I never would have expected to remind me of Grandpa that brings back my memory of a moment in time with him.'

MEMORY MOMENT! It was like Mind had made the greatest discovery in the world, and found the perfect name for it too.

Mind, now wrapped in fairy lights, pulled out the full length of cable to dig deeper into the box. Right at the bottom, Mind found some *diyas* from India. They were small clay lamps that we'd made with Grandpa and lit at Diwali time. Holding the *diyas* we had painted orange reminded us of Grandpa's favourite colour.

Suddenly, it was like we were standing

next to Grandpa again on his balcony, watching the sunset together, as he pointed his finger up and pretended he was painting the whole sky in the colour he loved the most. We heard him say:

'The day is getting on,
The setting sun has nearly gone.
It's left its bright colours behind,
In the sky and in your mind!'

'Maya!' Mama's voice brought Mind and me back from our MEMORY MOMENT.

'It's getting late and we've got an early start tomorrow.'

'I need to get all my sports stuff ready for Cricket Club after school tomorrow,' I reminded her.

Mind was behind me on this. Cricket was something that had always brought us closer to Grandpa and that was exactly what we needed now.

'Fine. Why don't you both put away the gardening equipment first and then we can eat . . .' Mama got planning. 'After we've eaten, we'll get your bag packed for school *and* we'll make sure you've got your sports uniform ready to wear for Cricket Club, so can we set off on time in the morning. You don't want to be late on your first day back!'

'I'll go get all the bits that need putting away and then we can look for your cricket gear. I'll be *right* back. Promise to stay put?' Papa looked at me with serious eyes.

I nodded.

'I'll wait here with Maya until you're back,' Mama squeezed the squishy bit of my hand gently with her thumb.

It was a rare moment of quiet one-to-one time with Mama, just me and her, no one and nothing else around to distract her. She was looking at me, listening to me, touching my hand, and felt close enough to smell me and even *taste* me (if I was a *chapatti*!).

I felt like asking her about the photograph of the little girl. But Mind didn't want to. Mind liked the mystery of it and thought we should keep something to ourselves.

It'll be more fun that way! Mind insisted.

Papa trundled back, scraping the heavy spade along the concrete path. He stopped to show off some of his best batting stances, sweeping and swinging it around like a bat. He got Mind and me so excited that we were sure he'd make the best cricket coach ever for our new Cricket Club at school tomorrow.

It didn't matter that we hadn't found Grandpa's cricket bat. Like Grandpa had told us when we were packing to move home: 'The memories you make, are all you need to take!'

We were about to make a bunch of new memories playing cricket that we could share with Grandpa in our next letter. Now that we'd remembered his favourite colour was orange, Mind had another bright idea – we could use orange paper as the perfect way to brighten Grandpa's day. The most important thing now, before we could get on with writing that letter, was to get our Cricket Club started!

CHAPTER 4

'Goood morning, MISTER DRODGE . . . Goood morrrrrning, every-one!' We all chanted in our school assembly the next morning.

It was the same line we started every lesson with, only swapping out the teacher's name and the time of day, depending on who it was and when. I liked it because I could belt it out as loud as I wanted to, and no one could tell my voice apart from the big group of everyone's voices. It was like mixing lots of different colours of paint together. Once the colour on your brush goes in, you can't really see it anymore. It all becomes one new colour that you never could have imagined until you made it; different every time, depending on which colours and how much of each goes into it.

There were hundreds of us in assembly, all sat cross-legged in neat rows that filled the sports hall. Mind knew some of the other children's names, but it was tricky to remember them all so I only ever spoke to my friends in my class.

Mind was still keeping a look out for Tanya and Anya – we hadn't seen them come in and it wasn't like them to be late. We would feel a lot better once they were here. It was like waiting for Papa to come home from work at night. It always felt better once we knew he was back, even if it was in the middle of the night. Mind always kept an ear out, even in our sleep, so we could hear Papa come in through the front door.

'Good morning, children!' Mr Drodge's voice blared out at us from the speakers on the ceiling.

Ever since he'd told us the name Drodge came from an old word for 'dragon', Mind imagined that, if he got cross enough at morning assembly, he'd turn into a dragon, breathing fire into the microphone and flapping his scaly wings to fan the flames higher. So, we tried to be on our best behaviour. Mr Drodge was the school Headteacher and also our Science teacher, so we had seen him lighting the flame of a Bunsen burner when he did experiments before in class that looked like magic to us. That made it seem all the more imaginable that he *could* secretly be a dragon with a mastery of fire.

Maybe all teachers are secretly dragons . . . Mind began to wonder, looking around the room at our teachers and picturing each one of them as a dragon. Each with their own DRAGONY personality and special skills that make them different to the others. That could explain why they all taught different subjects – maybe not all dragons are as good with fire?

Some are better with numbers, some better at reading books with us at story time. Mind made me chuckle.

Mrs Griffiths, an older dragon, peered at us suspiciously over gold-rimmed glasses that rested just above her nostrils. Mind saw a puff of magic dragon smoke around her nostrils as she flared them at us. Mrs Griffiths reminded Mind and me of the red dragon on the flag of Wales. Her name is Welsh and it means STRONG. That made me think of Grandpa. Just because he was old and his handwriting looked a bit untidy these days, it didn't mean he wasn't strong.

I reached into my pocket for his letter. It was a bit fiddly to open up without ripping it. The paper wasn't very strong, and the way Mind had folded and stuffed it in there in a hurry this morning didn't help.

At least I remembered to bring it along! Mind huffed.

'Maya' Mrs Griffiths puffed a plume of fiery smoke our way, 'Put that away please.'

'This morning, we have a *very* special announcement . . .' Mr Drodge declared.

This was it. Everyone was about to find

out about our new Cricket Club and they all had *me* to thank for it! Mind tidied me up, adjusting my shirt collar, picking some dried-up toothpaste off my jumper and brushing a couple of Pooey's hairs off my trousers.

Mr Drodge was definitely a friendly dragon. Unlike *Mr Strict* who was a ferocious dragon, with a look on his face all the time; as if you'd done something wrong and were going to be in some terrible trouble for it.

Mr Strict was *so* strict that *everyone* called him that . . . even the Headteacher, Mr Drodge!

'Now, I'll hand over to *Mr Strict*–' he coughed and corrected himself, 'Ah-hum! I mean . . . Mr Strickett.'

Giggles echoed around the hall, followed by hushes from the teachers sitting on benches at the back. As Mr Drodge walked off the stage, Mind saw him dragging his spiky dragon's tail between his legs in embarrassment.

'Good morning everyone.' Mr Strict inhaled sharply, like when there's a bad smell in the air that you're trying not to breathe in. It was as if greeting us was the last thing he wanted.

'Good morning, Mr Strict . . . Good morning everyone,' we all recited back politely, like trained parrots, following the rules to win star stickers (*polite* parrots, being the key to getting a star sticker). There are only two rules at school:

1. KIND WORDS.
2. KIND HANDS.

So, we have to be polite. That's why we say good morning and good afternoon back to our teachers and to everyone. Follow the rules and you get shiny star stickers on your chart. Sounds simple enough, doesn't it? But the truth is, it isn't simple at all because the real rules are different to the **R.E.A.L.** rules.

The **R.E.A.L.** rules are the ones no one told me about before I started school. I only found out about them in my first week at school, when a bigger kid took me aside in the playground, sat me down and told me all the ways I was going against the **R.E.A.L.** rules. I think she was trying to help but Mind wasn't so sure about that. She reeled them off like they were one of the first things you were supposed to ever learn. She knew them as well as I knew my ABCs!

R.E.A.L. rules are for the Cools

Everyone stays around their own part of the playground

After-school clubs are for the Bubs

Last ones to lunch, you get no bench

That last one always confuses Mind . . . *Who thought it was a good idea to rhyme the word lunch with bench?*

It was probably The Cools . . .

The Cools are basically the coolest group of kids, that the rest of us are supposed to want to be like to *fit in*. But Mind doesn't always want to fit in and be just like everyone else. Mind is one of a kind! So Mind has a habit of breaking the **R.E.A.L.** rules, which gets us into all sorts of bother at school! For example, no one would ever come up with an idea for a new after-school club because they're meant to be for babies (Bubs). And yet, here we are . . .

'We have a brand new after-school club to announce . . .' Mr Strict went on.

'Waaaaaahhh! I want my MA-MAAA!!!' Someone shrieked from the front row.

That's where the Bubs all sit in assembly. The Bubs are all the younger Year Ones, just like me a couple of years ago. There are two types of Bubs: the first type is shy and quiet, and the second type is confident and keen. When the twins started school, Anya was the first type and Tanya was the second type. Aunty Dolly was always trying to get Anya to go to after-school clubs, while Tanya was always trying to join yet another after-school club. I was a Bub once myself and I still remember how it felt when Mama would drop me off in the morning at the school gates. Mama and Papa even tried taking turns dropping me off, to see if it was less upsetting for me to have Papa take me to school. But that only made things worse ...

'If there are no more interruptions ...' Mr Strict gave the teachers a stern look, as if to say how awful it was that he had to start again and that it was all *their* fault. 'I shall continue ...'

Mr Strict always sounded so bored, it was very hard to not also feel bored listening to him. We'd probably be better off if he was actually a dragon. All the stories we'd ever read about dragons, described them as mystical creatures hidden away, sometimes in a magic castle, a cave or other lair: a place no one ever dares to go, except on a quest to save the Kingdom. That might explain why schools have secret places only for dragons (I mean, teachers), where no one else is allowed to go – like the *staff room*.

But don't dragons need to sleep for ages, sometimes hundreds of years . . . ? Mind made a good point.

We often heard our teachers telling each other they didn't get enough sleep and they do seem pretty grumpy some mornings . . . But then, so do all grown-ups.

Maybe ALL grown-ups are DRAGONS?! Mind gasped, springing up and hurling Grandpa's letter into the air.

'MIND!' I *whispouted* (that's what we call it when I think I've whispered something to

Mind but I've actually shouted it out loud).

Everyone in the rows ahead of us turned around. It felt like every single person in the hall was staring at us now. The Bubs in front of us, the Cools behind us, the dragons (I mean, teachers) all around us.

'Maya!' Mrs Griffiths got out of her chair and pulled me up by my hand to stand. She marched me straight out of the hall.

That's the other thing about the school rules ('kind words' and 'kind hands') – they don't always make sense. I hadn't been *un*-kind but here I was, in trouble anyway.

CHAPTER 5

RIIINNGGG!
RIIINNNGGG!!

The school bell rang through the whole building so loudly that it shook the walls, and went into my ears like it was ringing through my whole body too.

It was the last bell of the day. That meant it was home time (at least for the Cools) and time for after-school clubs for the Bubs ... and anyone else who cared to join them.

Part of me was excited. Papa would be here any moment now. Part of me felt nervous about hanging out with a group of kids I didn't know very well.

At least Tanya and Anya will be there! Mind hopped from one foot to the other, and then on all fours in a circle around my feet, just like Pooey when she thinks I've got carrots for her.

I hoped Tanya and Anya would get to the changing rooms before me, so I could go straight over to them and not have to worry about not knowing anyone there.

Then again, I didn't want to be late and miss the start of Cricket Club. We'd already missed the big announcement in assembly. Kids had been talking about it in class and in the playground all day. I got the sense that EVERYONE wanted to know more. Cricket wasn't something we did at school normally, which meant it was different.

To Mind, different meant *special*. It

was obvious that even some of the Cools sounded interested, while *trying* to sound *un*-interested (just so they were sticking to the R.E.A.L. rules on after-school clubs being for Bubs). For the first time since I started school, I was glad not to be one of the Cools. I could like whatever I wanted to like, unlike them! I didn't have to pretend. *Playing* pretend when we want to, is fun for Mind and me, but having to hide who you are and pretend to be *something else* all the time is, well . . . *something else!*

Sounds exhausting for them, Mind sighed, feeling sorry for the Cools, as we pushed open the heavy door to the changing room with plenty of energy of our own.

Inside, sat in the middle of the room, surrounded by lockers, and staring straight at me as I stepped in, was someone I never expected to see—

Beth the Bully! Mind stopped right there.

Beth is one of the Cools. She used to pick on me when I first started school here after we left India. Mind backed up and ran in reverse in a circle around me as my thoughts raced.

She was mean to me about so many things, like the Indian banana chips in my packed lunch because it was different to her packet of crisps.

At first, I didn't tell Mama about it because I knew it was already hard enough for her to get used to us living here. But when Tanya found out, she taught me how to stick up for myself, using *The Snarl*.

'If anyone's mean to you, you just use

The Snarl . . .' she told me, with the confidence of someone who had been at school much longer than me and had successfully used *The Snarl* as a survival skill.

'You make *this* face,' she pulled one side of her top lip up to her nose while squinting the eye on the same side. 'Then pull your finger back and point at them like you're jabbing air their way, and yell: *BACK OFF!*'

I'd practiced it loads of times, with and without Tanya showing me exactly how to do it. But I'd never had to put it into action, because Beth joined the Cools and stopped talking to me before I ever got a chance. I was just a Bub then, so not someone any of the Cools had any time for.

Mind still thought of her as *Beth the Bully*. But it had been so long since then, we were past all of that now, weren't we?

Seeing Beth here stirred up a mix of different feelings in me. All sorts of thoughts came to Mind. Mind poured some of them together into a pot, and gave it a stir—

A pinch of a problem from the past!

A smidgen of seeming unsure!

A dash of danger!

Then Mind dipped a finger into the broth and licked it. Something didn't taste right.

The Cools weren't *supposed* to join after-school clubs. So, what was Beth doing here?!

'Hiya Maya,' Beth gave me a half-smile. It felt natural to smile back but Mind was panicking and in a FLAP, wrapped around my head, squeezing my cheeks and holding them together so tight that I couldn't do a thing! Forget about using *The Snarl*.

Thankfully, just then, before I had to come up with something to say or do, the door swung open . . . Surely the next person to walk in had to be a Bub, someone to distract Beth.

Don't look NOW . . . It's Sara Rao! Mind blared like some kind of rhyming alarm, letting go of my cheeks, only to cover my eyes instead.

I peeled Mind's hands off my face. I *had* to see for myself. Sure enough, stood right there in front of me, was the one and only *Sportsday Superstar*. Having someone sporty in our Cricket Club had to be a GOOD thing – it was a sports club, after all – but then why did it feel so BAD to see her there?

Flappy Mind was working away at the mixture again, vigorously whisking in some more stuff but that only made it worse. Our thoughts and feelings were getting messier with every second. Mind studied the pot carefully, tilting it side to side, and sniffed the thick mix of thoughts and feelings, making a face. It wasn't like anything we'd seen (or smelt) before.

Look to the left: Beth the Bully! Mind turned my head one way and then the other. *Look to the right: Sportsday Superstar Sara!*

Things weren't looking great. I couldn't blame Mind for flapping . . . But *where* was Mind now?!

I looked up and saw Mind clinging to the ceiling, rubbing the mix of feelings from the pot all over like sunscreen. It was like a paste sticking to Mind, like frosting on a cake – except it hadn't ended up as a sweet feeling but a *sickly* one. That's when I realised I was about to be SICK! That was the last thing Mind needed. There had to be something or someone to help bring us back from what was about to turn into a MEGA FLAP.

Just then, like superheroes to the rescue, Tanya and Anya burst into the changing room, their jackets flapping behind them like capes.

'I'm baaa-aaack!!!' Tanya announced musically, standing tall with her chin up, shoulders back and both arms on her hips. She sprang forwards, like the plastic toy frog I'd got in my party bag from the twins at their birthday last year (chosen by Anya the Animal

Expert, naturally).

It smells like . . . BIRTHDAY . . . Mind smiled dreamily, holding the frog next to my nose so I could smell it too.

'*Everyone's* back, Tanya . . . It's the start of another school term . . . Everyone comes back after the holidays. That's just the way it works,' Anya mumbled, rolling her eyes at her sister and following her in.

I couldn't have been happier to see the two of them.

Imagine what their party bags will look like this year . . . Mind began to wonder, as they made their way in.

That distracted me from the sickly feeling before it took over completely. Tanya and Anya had saved me from throwing up.

I ran over to Anya and threw my arms around her. Mind wished our hug would last forever. Tanya was already off and away making friends with everyone who had trailed in while I was busy trying to keep up with Mind's flapping!

Tanya didn't seem nervous at all.

Before we knew it, the Sports teacher, Miss Wong, was blowing her whistle to get our attention.

'Sit down, children!'

Everyone found themselves a space on the bench. Even Mind wanted to listen in to what Miss Wong was about to tell us.

'Welcome to Cricket Club! As you know, we have never played cricket before so it's a first for the school. We are very grateful that a parent has kindly offered to be your coach.'

Tanya winked at me from across the room. It felt like everyone was staring at me but trying not to show it, so they weren't being rude.

'I'd like you to all give our new coach a very warm welcome!' Miss Wong started clapping and everyone joined in.

I clapped extra hard because it felt extra special to have *my* Papa lead *my* school Cricket Club that *my* Grandpa in India inspired me to start. I couldn't take my eyes off the door, as we watched and waited for Papa to enter, like a champion cricket player at a stadium walking out onto the field, to the sound of fans applauding.

I felt the excitement bubbling up and Mind floated out of my head like a light and bouncy bubble, **BOING BOING BOING!**

Then, the changing room doors opened more dramatically than EVER before. Mind was shocked by who appeared through the door. Not Papa, but instead, utterly unexpectedly and unbelievably . . .

MAMA?!

Mind was stunned into silence. I was speechless.

Not that it mattered. It wasn't like I could put my hand up and ask Mama in front of everyone why *she* had showed up and not Papa. Mind put a hand up instead . . . to burst the last few bubbles that were still in the air. One by one, they disappeared, and so too did the excited feeling they'd brought with them.

Tanya, on the other hand, looked thrilled to see Mama.

'That's *my* Aunty!' I heard her gossiping with the person next to her.

HEY! Why is Tanya sitting with Superstar Sara?! Mind noticed the two of them together. That was almost more shocking than the moment we saw Mama.

Why were Tanya and Superstar Sara (one of my most favourite people and one of my least favourite people!) acting like besties? Why was *Mama* acting like she was interested in cricket?? And why was *Beth the Bully* here at all???

All I knew, was that I had to *act* like I didn't care! Especially because Mind was acting like it was the end of the world!

CHAPTER 6

Mama took charge straight away, talking to us as if she was a real-life cricket coach for a top team and talking to news reporters from across the world, ahead of a big tournament.

'Thank you Miss Wong and thank you everyone. It is truly an honour to be here to coach new talent. We are about to embark upon something great together. Greatness takes great effort. So we have to be prepared to work hard. I am going to be the *best* coach, to the BEST team.'

The room was still.

Mind went from speechless to speechless

and sweaty. Mama was making us NERVOUS.

'I grew up in India . . .' She continued, her eyes fixed on a distant memory.

Mind had no idea where Mama was going with this. *It's not supposed to be a speech about her life. What on earth is she going to say next?!*

'. . . and I am about to tell you something very important I learned about cricket when I was a child . . .'

I dared to look around. It was hard to tell from everyone's expressions if anyone else was anywhere near as uncomfortable as Mind and me. Mama was being weird, but she'd got everyone's full attention.

'*Cricket* isn't just a game . . . it is a way of LIFE!'

Tanya stood up and started clapping. It wasn't long before everyone else was doing the same thing.

That really got Mama going:

'So, let's *live* it!'

'Yaaarrrrrhhh!' Miss Wong cheered her on with a dragon-like growl, her hands curled into fists.

'You gotta be *in it* to WIN IT . . . Innit?!' Mama was getting carried away now. 'From the moment you wake up every morning, to the moment you're ready to fall asleep at night, remember to THINK cricket, FEEL cricket and LIVE cricket!'

PHOOT! PHOOOT! PHOOOOOT! Miss Wong whistled in celebration. Tanya and Superstar Sara high fived each other.

'Are you with me?!'

I had no clue what Mama was talking about and what we were agreeing to, but it seemed like everyone else was *with her*.

Even Anya was joining in and clapping along politely.

'Now! We just need to choose a Captain for our team . . .' Miss Wong stopped whistling and suddenly sounded serious like Mama. 'Any volunteers? Hands up!'

Tanya's hand shot up faster than we could think. Superstar Sara's hand followed.

Everything was moving so quick. Mind couldn't keep up. We'd barely caught the words that Miss Wong was flinging our way like a flame-throwing dragon and the group had moved on!

'Two in the running . . . Who votes for Tanya as Captain?'

Mind didn't want us to miss out again, so pulled my arm up and waved my hand around like I was a puppet. Before I'd had a chance to figure out what was happening,

Miss Wong had counted the hands in the air, including mine thanks to Mind!

'Wow Tanya, looks like you're the Captain of our team!'

Everyone cheered. I frowned and Mind started to flap.

'Anyone else for Vice Captain? Otherwise it goes to Sara ...'

What was a *Vice* Captain, anyway?! I tried to think, but Mind couldn't bear Sara winning, like she always did.

'Anyone? Last chance ...'

Mind impatiently flapped two huge elephant ears at me and raised a trunk, signalling at me to raise my hand.

I put my hand up eventually, only to stop flappy elephant-Mind charging at me with two terrifying tusks.

'Ah, Maya's got her hand up!' Miss Wong announced, to my horror. 'Okay, the two of you, Sara and Maya: you can both share the job as Co-Vice Captains!' Miss Wong clapped.

Mind was de-flapping, trunk and tusks gone now. The paste from the mix of feelings had dried up and was starting to crack off Mind. Left behind was Mind with a strange green stain all over.

I looked over at Tanya and Sara. My tummy was full of a horrible feeling that I couldn't put a name to. They were busy laughing and patting each other on the back; too busy congratulating each other to look at me.

'Everyone – outside!' Mama ordered. 'Captain Tanya, lead the way!'

Tanya sped towards the playing field, with Sara by her side and everyone else following after. Except for me and Mind – left behind. My bottom was still on the exact same spot on the bench as it had been, BEFORE *Tanya* became Captain of the team in *my* Cricket Club that *I* had started. And *that* was exactly where we wanted to be: back there, BEFORE any of this happened.

The longer I looked at Mind, the more *green* Mind looked. Mind was changing colour from a light lettuce-y green to a serious spinach-y green, and was getting GREENER by the second! Dark green smoke began billowing out of the top of Mind's head. It was almost like Mind was turning into an angry, ginormous, steaming hot...

'BROCCOLI?!'

Err... NO. I'm the green-eyed monster!

'You *look* more like a green *veggie* than a green monster.'

The green-eyed monster shows up when you feel JEALOUSY. Not when you feel HUNGRY!

'Jealousy isn't really a monster, silly! It's a feeling inside you.'

Mind didn't like being corrected. Mind turned away in a great, green, GRUMP.

GRRRRGLE! It was my tummy again. This time, it wouldn't stop.

GRRRRGLEEE!!! GLAAARRHHH!!!

It felt like my stomach was about to turn inside-out! I ran into the toilets, just in case whatever was *inside* my tummy was about to make an appearance on the *outside* . . .

'Are you okay?' a voice interrupted me, mid-tummy rumble, and Mind, mid-flap.

It was Beth! Mind and I were in no state to come up with a cover up.

'I feel a bit sick,' I confessed.

Beth reached into her backpack, like she was reaching for her best bullying bric-a-brac. She pulled out . . . a packet of crisps.

Mind was on FULL ALERT: Ready and set to GO! Beth with crisps meant TROUBLE for us in the past. If *Beth the Bully* thought she could still pick on us, she was in for a surprise. Mind wasn't going to let her get away with it. This was our chance, at last . . . to pull out *The Snarl*.

But before we could say or do anything, Beth passed the pack to me.

'Sometimes when I feel sick, salt 'n'

vinegar crisps make me feel better.'

I wasn't sure what to say or do but it didn't feel like we needed to use *The Snarl*. Mind put it away and took the packet of crisps. Mind examined it suspiciously. I felt so sick I was willing to try *anything* at this point.

'I know they're not as cool as those banana chips you used to bring to school.' Beth smiled, then looked down and pointed at the packet in my hand. 'Sometimes you just need to eat something. I like the vinegary flavour.'

Vinegar?! Mind's ears turned less *green* and more *keen* at the sound of one of our favourite flavours. *We love vinegar with chips and dips, so why not in crisps?!*

We *had* to give it a go. Mind couldn't understand why *Beth the Bully* was being nice to us but went ahead and popped open the foil packet anyway. We bit into a couple of the biggest crisps we could find, with a super loud **CRUNCH!** The taste of vinegar tickled my tongue and grains of salt danced a jive inside my mouth.

'Wow!' I laughed with relief, after a few seconds. 'It really works – my sick feeling is all gone!'

Maybe Beth wasn't so bad after all. Mind felt a bit mean for still calling her *Beth the Bully.*

That wasn't exactly following the rules – kind words and kind hands – was it?

So I decided to try some kind words: 'Thanks, Beth.'

'No worries! Let's go, we don't want to miss out on your *cool* Cricket Club!'

Did one of the *Cools* just call my club COOL?! Beth took me by my hand (well, actually the wrist of my hand that was still holding the packet of crisps) and she led us out of the toilets and changing rooms.

Mama had NEVER shown *any* interest in cricket before – at least, not to us! I couldn't have guessed in a million years that Mama would end up being the coach of our school team . . . OR that we'd *ever* be running hand-in-hand like buddies with an old enemy. *Beth* had gone from *Bully* to *Buddy!*

It was only our first day of Cricket Club and already miracles were happening! What could possibly happen next?!

The door swung open. Outside, it was like someone had painted the sky grey. Heavy clouds were hanging over the field. We felt droplets of rain on our faces, only the lightest of touches at first.

Then, almost immediately, the rain poured harder, like someone playing a xylophone with a mallet on top of our heads. In the distance, we could just about make out the dark specks of everyone dotted along the horizon. They were almost like the musical notes we'd seen on the sheet music that Mrs Menon used to play on the piano in school assemblies, before she retired. RETIRED. That was a word we hadn't thought of in a while.

Retired . . . retired . . . retired . . . Mind repeated the word, and paced around in a circle on the wet grass, trying to recall how we knew it.

That's when Mind had another MEMORY MOMENT!

When did we first hear the word *retired*? Years ago!

Where were we at the time? India!

Who were we with? GRANDPA!

Mind turned into a giant clock-face with hands turning backwards, taking us WAY back in time . . .

. . . it was years ago in India when we were with Grandpa. He was telling us about his job as a pilot flying planes, and I said I wanted to fly just like him. He laughed and the skin around his eyes crinkled up with lines that went all the way down his cheeks. *I want to go flying with you, Grandpa!* He lifted me up in the air and I put my arms out like the wings of a plane. That was when everyone in our family started calling me *Maya the Flyer!*

Grandpa wished he could take me flying, but he'd stopped working when he had grandchildren so he could spend more time at home with us – he RETIRED from his job. So, instead he taught me how to make paper airplanes, and lifted me high up in the air so we could fly together around the house. So . . . it was GRANDPA who had taught us the word 'retired', and along with it he gave us that special memory of us flying in his arms.

CHAPTER 7

The next morning, my eyes blinked open to the blurry sight and muffled sound of SHUFFLING in my room. Mind was still half-asleep, while I tried to figure out what was going on. It wasn't Pooey rustling in her hutch. This was something or someone taller, not as rustle-y as Pooey and a lot less rabbity.

I rubbed my eyes to clear out the sticky sleep from them. A few blinks later, I saw . . . with both arms stretched up as high as they could reach, standing on a stool, and trying to put something up on the inside of my bedroom door . . . Mama!

No chance of a lie-in, then! Mind yawned. *A lion? RARR!* Mind turned into a lion cub and pounced out of bed.

As Mama managed to get the top corners to stick with what looked like tape, a huge poster rolled open. I recognised the Captain of the England Women's Cricket Team right off the bat!

But it only made me wish Tanya wasn't Captain and that *I* was. That seemed unkind to Mind, who was licking a furry paw. After all, I should be proud of my family, in the same way I hoped they would be proud of me for starting Cricket Club in the first place. *Thinking* about it, that made perfect sense. But it didn't match how I *felt*.

Lion-cub-Mind spotted the three lions on the England cricket crest in the picture, and stood tall and proud. I imagined myself standing there proudly too, bat in hand, ready to lead my team to victory.

Then, I thought I recognised where the picture on the poster was taken . . . Mind went pirouetting around and around like a spinning top, back in time again . . . for another MEMORY MOMENT!

When did we first see that stadium? The Cricket World Cup!

Where were we at the time? India!

Who were we with? GRANDPA!

We had to get going!

We didn't want to be late for school. We couldn't afford to be in trouble *again* today.

Mind did what we always did when we woke up: hopped over to Pooey's hutch to check if she was up and ready to hop out herself. Out of all the jobs Mama and Papa made me do around the house now that I was a Big Kid, taking Pooey out to the garden to play in the morning was my *favourite*. But Pooey was nowhere to be seen! And we hadn't heard her rustling in the hay like she usually does when she wakes up. Surely Pooey hadn't gone missing *again?!*

'Pooey . . . ?' I kneeled down to open her hutch door, hoping she was there.

'Oh, don't worry about things like that!' Mama brushed past me, to put another poster up over my bookshelf, shaking it open like she was hanging wet laundry out to dry, and seemingly ignoring the fact that she was covering the shelves and all my books. This time, it was the India Women's Cricket team, all dressed in blue, my favourite colour.

'I already put Pooey out in her playpen in the garden this morning, so that you and I can focus on the one thing that needs our full attention ... CRICKET!'

Mama didn't stop for a moment, moving around my room non-stop, like an ant marching this way, then that way, keeping on going no matter what got in the way. This time, she pushed past us to get to the skylight above my bed. 'Papa's going to run you through some training drills this morning and then he'll drop you off at school. I need to go in early to work on our strategy for the team, ahead of the big announcement I'll be making at Cricket Club after school today.'

Not ANOTHER big announcement . . .

Mind grimaced.

Yesterday's big announcements really hadn't gone our way and Mind wasn't looking forward to any more *annoying* announcements.

Mama stuck a poster over the skylight, blocking out all the light. The room became as gloomy as Mind felt about facing another Cricket Club announcement.

'See you there!' Mama winked cheerfully, completely clueless about how she was coming across.

There was no *have a nice day!* or *love you!* or kiss goodbye. She didn't seem *bothered* about whether I brushed my teeth or combed my hair either! She didn't seem to *care* if I was hungry or thirsty ... forget about making me breakfast!

'*Frühstücken?*' She *did* remember breakfast for me, after all. I nodded with a smile – she *did* care!

Mama pulled out a red apple and I caught it with both hands. It was hardly the sort of *breakfast* we were imagining ...

'Gotta practice that catch for when you're out in the field!'

Mega-Coach Mama is ALL about CRICKET! Mind groaned.

Mega-Coach Mama had just one thing on her mind, day and night ... CRICKET! If that wasn't bad enough, she was being *pushy* about it. It was like she didn't even notice us anymore.

At least we can check on Pooey outside ... Mind tried to look on the bright side.

'Oh, and no playing with Pooey!' Mama nudged me along with the end of a rolled-up poster. 'Don't want that *mind* of yours getting distracted ...' she bopped me on top of my head with the roll. 'Cricket, cricket, cricket!'

Normally, I loved being with Mama, even if she was busy. It felt good to be in the same room as her. I especially loved it when she came up to my room to play and for storytime. But it wasn't very nice to be around *this* Mama, because she wasn't being like Mama at all. I was starting to wish she would stay away from my room. Who knew what she would do next?

KRRRRRRCHHH!

I turned around, and was horrified to find Mind balancing dangerously on tippy toes at the end of my bed, trying to peel a corner of one of the posters off the ceiling and tearing the wallpaper off with it! It was my favourite wallpaper in the whole house. I couldn't BELIEVE that Mama would cover it up without telling me.

And I couldn't BEAR to see it getting torn off like that.

'Stop!' I pulled Mind away from the poster and took us down the stairs. 'Let's just GO!'

When we first moved here, I missed India so much that Mama and Papa let me pick my very own special flowery wallpaper for my room, as a way to help cheer me up about having a new room, in our new house, in a part of the world that was new to me. We made a sign on the door, with Papa's special saying written on it, that always made me feel better: *Vielen Dank, für die Blumen!* Thank you for the flowers!

I looked back at my room from the top of the stairs, but Mama had covered the sign on the door with a poster of the England Women's Cricket team. I had to catch and stop Mind from turning into a flapping chinchilla, bolting back towards the bedroom door. Mind wanted nothing more than to rip off all the posters right away with those tiny chinchilla claws and CANCEL CRICKET CLUB.

Mama has taken things too far!

But, seeing the whole England team together, all the team members side by side for their big group photo, reminded me we were doing this for our TEAM. It wasn't just about Mind and me, anymore.

So, after school, yet again, we found ourselves back in the changing rooms, waiting with the rest of the team for Mama to arrive to make her big announcement. I would have much rather forgotten about it by now, but it was the only reason Mind was still here: for the team (and feeling a tad curious now about this *mysterious* announcement). We wondered if

Miss Wong was in on it. She looked a bit stressed, checking her watch over and over. Where *was* Mama? It wasn't like Mega-Coach Mama to be even a minute late for Cricket Club. Maybe she had transformed back into our Mama from before Cricket Club ever began. *That* Mama was almost *always* late.

BAAAAAAM!

Mama burst out of the tall metal cupboard between the lockers, catching us all out. It was so unexpected, she even made Miss Wong jump out of her seat.

'SURRR-PRISE!!!' she warbled at us with a gleeful glint in her eyes. 'Today's announcement is going to be the biggest and best SHOCK you've *ever* had!'

'Whoaaaa . . . What an entry . . .' Tanya looked impressed.

'And that's not the only ENTRY you're going to be thinking about when you leave here today . . .' Mama strode around the room, like a performing magician trying to get everyone's attention and draw in a crowd before she did her top trick. Everyone looked dazzled.

'I have entered our team into our first ever cricket match!'

'YES!!!' Tanya leapt into the air.

'We, the Shooting Stars, will *face-off* . . .'

'Ahem!' Miss Wong interrupted disapprovingly.

Mama paused and tried to come up with a better way to say what she had to say. 'We, the Shooting Stars, will go *head-to-head* . . .'

Miss Wong faked a cough and shook her head at Mama.

'Fine.' Mama rolled her eyes and kept it short and sweet. 'We're going to play another school team called the Sixer Strikers.'

When? Where?? Why??? Mind just about managed, before getting in a flap.

We hadn't even seen the other team, but they already sounded better than us. They had the words *sixer* and *strikers* in their team name, which made Mind and me think they were probably experts at striking sixers. I'd never hit a sixer in my life.

'Sports Day is right around the corner and the perfect chance for us to show off our new team to the whole, wide, world!' Mama was really getting into it now.

Sports Day?! But that's only THREE DAYS away!!! Mind sprouted a pair of goat horns and four hooves.

'What better way to celebrate the successful start of our Cricket Club? So, get yourselves ready for the big game, spread the word, shout out about it to everyone you know ... Let the countdown begin to our debut match on home turf, this spectacular Sports Day!'

That's when Mind started to *flap* like a panicked goat that needed to pee, right now!

'Three days to go – let's make a PLAN!' Tanya joined Mama in the middle of the room.

We don't need a plan, we need a pee! With one especially high jump-kick, Mind's horns caught the corner of a box on the top shelf, flinging multi-coloured clothes pegs across the room.

'Oh wowww!!!' Tanya lunged forward trying to collect them as they rained down. 'Rainbow clips for my Captain's cap!'

I was just glad it was a spray of pegs and not pee showering over everyone.

Anya, meanwhile, spotted a woodlouse shuffling out from under the box that needed saving.

I held Mind by the hoof and off we went to pee. 'Let's GO!!!'

CHAPTER 8

'GO! GOO!! GOOO!!!' Mama shouted as she led us, like a farmer leading goats, across the train station.

Her words echoed down the staircase that led, not to a farm, but to the platform where our train was due to arrive any minute.

'Yes, but NO running, *kids*!' Miss Wong from behind us, nervously checking every instruction Mama gave us. 'It's too *wet* and *slippy* for your little hooves . . . I mean, feet!'

She sounded just like the teachers at my swimming class, when they reminded us not to run by the pool. But, there was no swimming pool here. There were signs everywhere to remind passengers of the HAZARDS all around. A couple of strangers sprinted, one of them almost skidding into a bin. We didn't want to miss our train, but if we got hurt we might end up missing our train *and* Sports Day.

Gotta be IN IT to WIN IT! One of Mama's cheesy one-liners came to Mind.

There were no puddles anywhere, because the platform was so even and smooth that it was wet everywhere. I looked back at our footprints in the rainwater on the concrete. The ones furthest away had faded. I watched the last footsteps disappear. Just like my memories of India and of Grandpa, they were going, *going* . . .

GONE!

I had been so busy with Cricket Club, thinking it would help me remember Grandpa from when we used to play cricket with him, that I still hadn't gotten around to writing my letter to him. The one thing that had always kept us connected was writing letters to each other. And yet here we were: no *closer* to sending Grandpa a letter *and* not feeling any *closer* to Grandpa through playing cricket like I'd hoped. It wasn't just *my* fault, though: Mega-Coach Mama couldn't spare even a moment away from coaching us to help me write my letter.

But . . . what about all of our MEMORY MOMENTS? Mind reminded me, frantically putting them together like pieces of a puzzle.

We had collected quite a few and, as time went by, the more we thought about

Grandpa the more our memories of him were starting to come together. There were so many pieces still missing, we had to keep going! If we could finish the puzzle, we were sure to feel closer to Grandpa. And IMAGINE if we won the Sports Day match. We could write all about it in our letter to Grandpa. He would be so proud of us!

Plus, once Sports Day is over, we'll have time to sit down with Mama to write our letter . . .

Mind was right – whether we liked it or not, we needed Mama's help to write a letter in Hindi. But there was no point bringing it up here and now . . . She was in full-on Mega-Coach Mama mode.

'We don't want to waste any time, team! So on our train ride, let's all practice our bowling grip . . .' She walked down the aisle in the middle of our seats, handing us a red apple each, as if it was a cricket ball.

Tanya tossed her apple straight up and caught it.

'Yes, but *no throwing*, children!' Miss Wong reminded us, anxiously watching for what Mama might say or do next.

Mind wondered if Miss Wong had had enough of Mega-Coach Mama too.

'Equally important . . .' Mama added, as

she took her seat. 'No eating!'

'Awh!' Tanya protested, taking her apple out of her mouth and plonking it on her table.

'These apples are for *practising* your *grip!*' Mama scolded.

Tanya gripped her apple tightly and rubbed her thumb over the side with bite marks in it.

'Typical Tanya . . . doing everything we're *not* supposed to,' Anya complained to me. 'Makes you wonder why *she's* Captain.'

It wasn't like Anya to be jealous of Tanya. Mind wasn't sure what to make of Anya's comment or how to react, but it definitely helped me feel less guilty. Of course, feeling jealous didn't mean Mind was turning into a monster! We just had lots of different feelings just like Anya, and just like everyone else.

Mama stood up and went to the front of the carriage, where we could all see and hear her.

'Listen up, everyone – time for a Team Talk!'

Mind couldn't take many more of Mega-Coach Mama's Team Talks, as she liked to call them. Neither could I. They always seemed to end up in Mind flapping. I wasn't sure I could manage Mind in a flap on a fast-moving train!

'Ahead of our big Sports Day match, I've devised a brand new format of the game . . . It's an action-packed day for the school, so we need to make it short enough to fit in. So, I present to you all . . .'

She unfolded a large sheet of sugar paper with a drawing of a cricket pitch and field, with star stickers for the players dotted around.

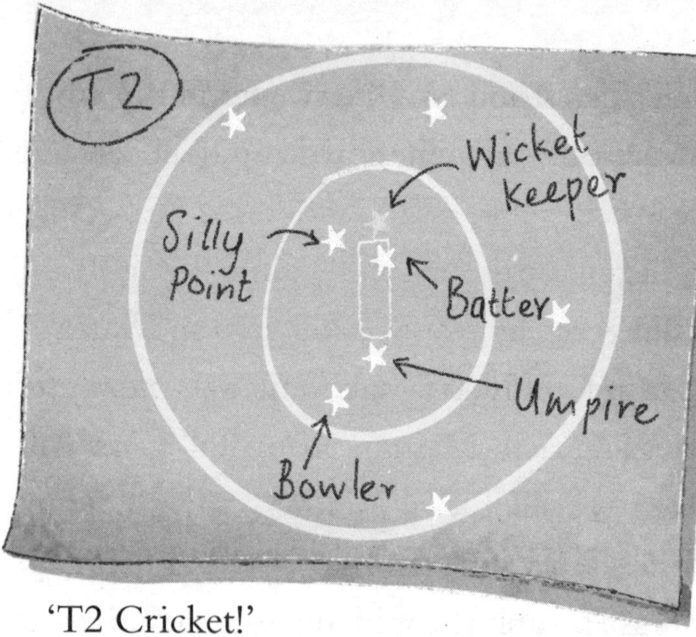
T2
Wicket
Keeper
Silly
Point
Batter
Umpire
Bowler

'T2 Cricket!'

It had a nice ring to it. But Mind wondered what it meant. We'd heard of Twenty20, or T20, cricket. That was a shorter game than other types of cricket that can go on for DAYS! But this *T2 Cricket* sounded like something Mama just made up by herself.

'It's the fastest paced and most thrilling game of cricket you could ever imagine, which means, as players, you've got to think quick and be fast on your feet!'

She rolled the sheet back up like a yo-yo, popped a rubber band around it again and tossed it towards us.

Tanya sprung out of her seat and caught it so smoothly, it was almost like we were watching a brilliantly rehearsed game of Frisbee.

'Excellent work, Cap'n!' Sara winked at Tanya as she passed her the roll, like a baton in a relay race.

Mind was starting to get jittery about the whole thing. If Mega-Coach Mama's shock news about the competition wasn't enough to get us feeling nervous, all the reminders of Sports Day certainly had us rattled. Put the two together and it was the perfect recipe for a FLAP ...

Did someone say FLAPJACK?! Mind still saw the funny side of it all, and that helped us relax a bit.

If only there was an actual flapjack in our snack pack, instead of another one of Mega-Coach Mama's *Training Treats* . . .

Ever since we'd started Cricket Club, she only packed us high-energy sports snacks, or Training Treats, as she called them.

'Each team has one innings. That's when it's your turn to bat and score as many runs as you possibly can, just like any game of cricket. But, what is UNIQUE about T2 Cricket is *this* . . .'

game plan! T2 shooting stars
Balls per Over = 6 × 2 (overs) → 12 balls
Time per Innings Over = 2½ mins × 2 (overs)
5 mins + 10 min break / 5 mins

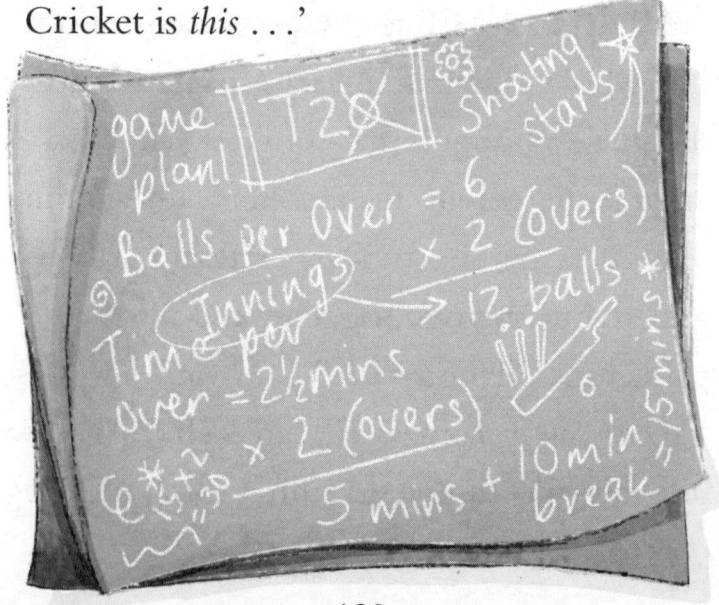

She unravelled another roll of sugar paper with lots of confusing numbers and letters all over it.

'The batting team only gets 12 balls bowled to them. By my calculation, the game will last about 20 minutes from start to finish.'

Mind wasn't very good at telling time yet, but 20 minutes didn't sound like long enough to play a full game of cricket. Then again, it was clear to see from the sheets of Mama's working that she had spent a LOT of time figuring everything out.

'I've factored in an official 10-minute break, when we will re-group and think about our strategy to secure the win!'

It was obvious to Mind and me just how much hard work and effort Mama was putting in to everything she was doing for us as our Coach. She had planned this field trip, and got everyone in our team special permission from their parents to take us to the rooftop nets at the gigantic sports centre in the city.

It was the biggest thing to happen at Cricket Club so far, and felt like something only the very Big Kids at school would normally get to do. So, I was thankful for that, even if nothing else was going our way. Mind pushed the nut and seed energy bar back into its packet after a quick sniff (it smelt like cardboard!).

When we finally got to the nets, it wasn't anything like we'd imagined. It was a wet and sticky evening, with bugs buzzing around our ears and moths mingling overhead. The sun started to set and lights on the walls flickered on.

I was up first. Mega-Coach Mama rolled

a ball my way. Mind was still warming up and instead of hitting the ball, my bat clunked clumsily against the floor.

'You're not bringing the bat up in time!' she yelled out loud enough for me (and everyone else around us) to hear.

'I think that bat's too heavy,' I heard Tanya nattering with the others, as she waited for her turn.

'Lift, Maya, lift! Like Grandpa showed you how to when you were little!' Mama was trying her best to help.

But it was so *embarrassing!* Mind had turned almost as dark red as the cricket ball by the time we were done.

Tanya's turn went so smoothly. She was as slick as a batter can be, whacking ball after ball into the nets and getting comments that I definitely didn't get:

'Niiiiice one!'

'Goooo on!'

'Ooohhh that's a jaffa!'

Mind stomped off, kicking a couple of balls that were lying around and steaming up like a boiling kettle. *What's a JAFFA anyway?!* But I knew this wasn't about the jaffa (whatever one of those was).

Whether we liked it or not (and Mind *didn't* like it one bit) the truth was: Tanya was WAY better at cricket than Mind and me, even when we were working together and giving it our best effort.

I put one hand on Mind's shoulder, trying to help us feel better. That's when I noticed my palms had changed colour, to . . . green!

Now YOU'RE turning into the GREEN-EYED MONSTER! Mind started to flap and grew a crocodile's tail to slap the green off the palms of my hands with.

SNAP! SNAP! SNAP! Crocodile-Mind went, flapping like never before. I skidded away and planted my bottom onto a bench, mainly to avoid getting an arm chomped off but also to take a moment to myself.

Mind spun around in circles, too busy chasing that scaly tail to follow me. I took a closer look at the green marks on the palms of my hands.

'Oh, don't worry,' Anya sidled up to me. 'Those are just grass stains – I've got them too.' She put both hands up and gave me a high ten.

THAPPP!!!

Tanya's bat smashed the ball our way. Crocodile Mind waddled over, tail jiggling behind.

'Wow what a WINNER!' Mega-Coach Mama called out.

Mind couldn't be sure whether she meant Tanya or her shot.

'I guess *that's* why Tanya's Captain!' Anya shrugged, nibbling on a whole carrot, just like a rabbit. 'I wouldn't want to be Captain, anyway. Would *you?*'

Anya's question got Mind and me wondering . . . Why did it even matter who was Captain?

The way Anya held onto her carrot with both hands and bit into the top of it reminded me of Pooey. Thinking about it, I hadn't seen

Pooey all day long. I definitely wouldn't get to play with her when we got home. It would be well past her bedtime – and *ours!* Mega-Coach Mama had taken Cricket Club too far and it was all getting a bit much for Mind and me. She was forgetting about the things that really mattered and so were we! Like Grandpa's letter, making memories together, and now even POOEY!

We'd had enough.

Tomorrow morning, after a good night's sleep, I was going to tell Mama everything. I didn't want to play cricket anymore. No more Cricket Club for Mind and me. Mind's scales peeled off and the crocodile snout and tail disappeared. That was when I knew for sure: I had to do what felt right for Mind and me. Having a cranky croc creeping around wasn't good for anybody!

CHAPTER 9

Look East or West ... Maya is the BEST!

Mind knew we were asleep and dreaming but Mind LOVES a good rhyme – and *this* was our favourite rhyming chant from that Cricket Cup final we had been to all those years ago in India with Grandpa.

Look East or West ... Maya is the BEST!!!

What a rhyme and what a dream! I was standing at the wicket, fully geared up from head to toe in batting equipment – helmet, chest guard, elbow pads, leg pads and spikes on my shoes. Oh, and not to forget the most important thing of all . . . my BAT! I looked and *felt* like a superhero.

It was our big moment – standing at one end of the pitch, ready to bat. The moment of our dreams . . . actually in a dream!

The ball spun my way and I moved to swing at it with my bat. But suddenly the bat was too heavy. It was like someone had superglued the end of my bat to the ground!

NEERRRGGHHH . . .

I grunted, straining to pull my bat away from the ground. Even Mind came over to help and tried pushing it up from underneath me.

No luck . . . it's STUCK!

Everything was against us, even forces we couldn't see or hear, like GRAVITY!

The wicket EXPLODED as the ball struck the stumps and the bails flew off. The green-eyed monster lurched towards us and teased me, sticking its fingers in its ears and tongue out at me.

"Na-na-na-na-na-naaah! You'll never be CAPTAIN!"

'MAMAAAAA!' I cried out, waking up soaked in my own sweat, from what had turned into a nasty nightmare.

I clambered out of bed and to the top of the staircase, Mind still looking for Mama.

'I've been meaning to talk to you about that . . .' I heard Papa's voice.

'Go for it!' came Mama's reply.

They were downstairs in the kitchen, talking like they did every night, while doing the dishes and laundry. I usually listened in secretly from the top of the staircase with Mind, but had fallen asleep on our way home last night, exhausted from batting practice. We took our usual seats, and pushed our feet through the gaps between the rails, Mind and me.

It was like going to the cinema. The kitchen night-talk versions of Mama and Papa were usually much more dramatic than they were in normal day-to-day life. Mama and Papa didn't realise we could hear *everything*. They were busy starring in their very own live-action sound-only movie of Life.

'You've been pushing Maya pretty hard.'

'Ssssshhhhhhhhhh . . .' Mama hushed him and closed the door to the kitchen.

Mind turned my head and cupped a hand around my ear, so we could still hear what they were saying. This was getting GOOD!

'There's no point shushing me. You know it's true. We've all had enough.'

It wasn't WHAT Papa was saying, but the WAY he was saying it: it wasn't kind. If previous kitchen night-talks were anything to go by, *that* was not going to go down very well with Mama.

Silence . . .

It went so quiet that we could hear Mama turning on the gas stove and slapping *chapatti* dough between her fingers.

No answer from Mama, meant one thing... *drama.*

Mind was biting my nails and couldn't take it any longer. *Someone say something...ANYTHING!*

Finally... thankfully... Mama spoke. 'Do you know *why* I'm doing all of this?'

I could hear her rolling out a *chapatti* with her wooden rolling pin against the stone worktop.

Now it was Papa's turn to stay quiet.

'Don't you think I *know* Maya calls me *Mega-Coach Mama*...'

Mind, mortified, slid away under the rug on the landing.

I could hear the hot air filling the *chapatti* like a balloon and cooking it all the way through, as Mama turned it over and then whipped it off the *tawaa* and onto a plate, before rolling another ball of dough ready to make the next one.

'Every time I roll a ball of *chapatti* dough between my hands, I *dream* of lobbing it across a cricket pitch, out on a grassy playing field . . .'

I imagined Papa looking gobsmacked, like Mind.

'*My* dream, ever since *I* was a little girl growing up in India . . . if anyone cares to know . . . was to play cricket. I was very talented and could have been a top player. Who knows, maybe I would have ended up playing for a national team. If only I'd had a coach who cared enough to encourage and *push* me, as you call it, to reach my dream.

Dreams don't come easily. You have to work *hard* to make your dreams come true. I was never allowed to play cricket seriously because there was no Women's team when I was younger. Maya's Grandpa had no choice when I was little, but I could never let my own daughter miss out like that . . .'

Mama's voice tailed off at the end and broke up, followed by snuffles that quickly became muffled, as we imagined Papa giving her a big hug.

'I didn't realise it meant so much to you,' Papa said kindly. 'Here, let me make that next *chapatti* . . .'

'I didn't realise I was pushing the girls so hard,' Mama responded rather sensibly.

We much preferred this to the kitchen night-talks that turned into little squabbles. Either way though, it was special for Mind and me to hear Mama and Papa taking time to talk to each other every night, about what they really felt deep down inside their hearts. They always made up in the end and stuck together, like the best team ever.

So much for our plans to QUIT our own cricket team! I guess we're gonna have to ride this one out . . .

Mind was back on board. I agreed with Mind. If I'd known Cricket Club meant so much to Mama, I would have practiced more. I definitely wouldn't have called her names like *Mega-Coach Mama.*

'I just wanted to make my parents proud,' Mama sniffed.

I was close to tears at the sound of hers.

The only time I'd seen Mama cry was when we left India, just after she said goodbye to Grandpa for the last time and we left his house. It was night-time and so dark in the taxi on the way to the airport that she probably thought I couldn't see. But the street lamps lit the side of her face, just enough for me to catch a glimpse. The instant I saw tears in her eyes, tears came to mine too.

'Who knows if he even remembers anymore,' she said to Papa as he flattened a *chapatti* dough ball between his fingers.

Why wouldn't Grandpa remember? Mind was baffled. Grandpa had always had the best memory in our family. He was the only one who remembered everyone's birthdays every year, without any screens to remind him. Everyone forgets things sometimes – none of us could remember where we'd kept Grandpa's cricket bat! And I couldn't even remember where I'd put Grandpa's last letter.

For a moment, an awful thought made Mind yelp: what if our forgetting to write back to him meant he was forgetting us too?

'Well, his memory isn't what it used to be. You know he hasn't been in the best of health this past year,' Papa said.

'Sssssshhhhhhhh . . . ! Maya *suneygi* . . .'

What did Mama not want me to hear? Mind was ALL EARS.

'We all know he's been in and out of the . . . *Krankenhaus* . . . at least *doh baar iss saal*.'

WHERE had Grandpa been in and out of at least twice this year?!

Mind scanned all our German words like flipping through the thin pages of Papa's German dictionary but we found *nothing*.
The word *Krankenhaus* was new to us.

'Try not to push yourself too hard to get everything perfect.'

'Try not to push that *chapatti* too hard, or it'll just get squished and turn out as crisp as a *poppadum!*' Mama couldn't help herself, trying to get things just right all the time. 'I do hope I haven't pushed the girls too hard.'

'At least they'll have some down time over the weekend with Tanya and Anya at their birthday party,' Papa tried to stay upbeat.

'And they'll get some kind of *bowling*

practice in at the bowling alley ahead of the big cricket match!' Mama laughed.

Papa must have raised his bushy eyebrows at her, as she quickly said, 'Okay. Sorry. I'll *try* to control myself . . . But only if you promise to take it down a notch with your carroty competitiveness.'

'DEAL!'

I loved hearing Mama and Papa talking to each other when no one else was listening (apart from Mind and me!). They were like best friends in a playground, picking each other up when one fell down and got hurt.

CRASSHHHH!

Uh oh! Mind had fallen over in the dark, on the way out of my room.

Loooook! Mind shoved the envelope with Grandpa's letter in it into my face, and opened the flap.

Mind took out the black and white

photo we'd found in the garden shed.

Don't you see???
THAT'S MAMA!

I took a closer look at the little girl playing cricket. It was hard to tell but the more I thought about it, the more I could see it was her. *And* she was holding what looked *exactly* like Grandpa's lucky bat! That's when I knew, it *had* to be her in the picture. It was the first time we'd ever seen Mama not as Mama, but as a person of her own before she became Mama; someone *we* had never met. She had a whole life of her own before we came along.

CRAAASSHHHH!!!

More stuff came crashing down in my room like an avalanche, off the shelf Mind had snatched the envelope from carelessly while rushing to show me the old photo. Mind was excited to have solved the mystery of the unknown girl.

What a night it had been, with Mind and me waking halfway through a bad dream at the start, and then Mama sharing her own dreams by the end. It really was time for us to get back to bed.

'Maya?' Papa called, as he ran towards the staircase to check if I was up. *'Ist sie wach?'*

Mind tugged at my pigtails, urging us to get back to my room before Papa saw us. But I couldn't move. It wasn't like in my dream, when my bat was stuck to the ground. I couldn't stop thinking about what I'd just seen, even for a moment, to think about anything else – like getting out of sight!

Mind was blown away by all the new information and floated into bed, where it seemed safest to hide away from everything we didn't want to face. As comfy as Mind looked, all cosy under the blanket, I wasn't going to run (or float) away. Not this time.

Papa switched on the light, and found me on the landing curled up, hugging my knees tight to my chest and my chin resting on top of them. I didn't look at him straight away. I didn't know what to say or do.

'Maya, why aren't you in bed?' He asked gently, sitting on the floor next to me. 'Did you have a bad dream?'

I nodded, as much as I could without

my jaw knocking into my knees.

'Aw, sorry to hear that,' he put his hand on my head and stroked my pigtails back into place. 'Do you want to talk about it?'

I shook my head.

'That's okay. Sometimes it's good to talk but sometimes it's good to just sit, *saath saath*.'

He was right. To start with, I just wanted to sit together. Even Mind thought about joining us, leaning out of bed a little bit.

After a few moments of quiet, Papa offered some words: 'I've missed spending time with you.'

'Me too!' I replied, relieved that it wasn't just me who felt that way.

Mind slinked out of my room and crawled over to us like a baby. I let go of my knees, sat cross-legged and cradled Mind.

'I know Mama's been really busy trying

to coach the cricket team. It's only because she cares so much. I've been extra busy with long days at work. It's an *über* busy time. But we *always* have time for you, no matter what else is going on.'

Mind seemed soothed by Papa's soft words, like a lullaby, and was starting to fall asleep in my rocking arms.

'Is there anything you want to ask me?' Papa sounded a bit worried himself, in case I'd heard what he and Mama were talking about in the kitchen. Truthfully, I had LOADS of questions. Like, what does *Krankenhaus* mean? And, what's a jaffa?! But I didn't want Mama and Papa to find out that listening in to their kitchen conversations from the top of the stairs was something we did from time to time. It was our only way to get the inside story and find out what was *really* going on sometimes.

BEH! Mind let out a broccoli breath baby burp and snuggled deeper in to me, feeling sleepier than I'd realised.

'Is there really no green-eyed monster?' I uttered, almost asleep, as Papa carried us back to bed.

'There are *no* monsters, Maya. They're just tricky feelings that everyone feels sometimes. Talking about how we feel can help us feel better again.'

He kissed the top of my head good night and wished me to sleep with every language he knew, like making three wishes with a genie's lamp –

'*Soh jah* . . . Sweet dreams . . . *Gute Nacht.*'

CHAPTER 10

Aaahhh! Mind's face wrinkled into a smile as we woke to the smell of fresh baking.

I ran to the top of the stairs and called out, 'Morning, Mama! Something smells *really* GOOD!'

'I thought you girls would enjoy decorating some cupcakes for us to take along to the birthday party this afternoon,' Mama came to the bottom of the stairs to see me and she put her arms out.

I climbed down and straight into a cuddle.

Mmm-mmmm! Now THAT'S more like it. Mind couldn't wait to get some icing and sprinkles on those cupcakes, rubbing both hands together in delight. And I couldn't have been more delighted to have my Mama *back*.

'How *very* odd . . .' Papa peeked through a gap between the curtains. 'The Rao's have parked up at our house instead of theirs across the road . . . Suppose I'd better go outside and say hello, to be polite – before politely reminding them that this isn't their driveway ...'

Papa put his hand out, reaching for mine, 'Let's go, we *are* neighbours, after all!'

Mind didn't move.

We already had to see Sara Rao EVERY DAY of the week, for after-school cricket practice. Today was the start of our weekend. That meant *no* Cricket Club and *no* Rao's today.

Week End = END of the WEEK. It's meant to be a break!

'Wonder what they're thinking, blocking our car in like that,' Papa moaned.

What if we ended up getting late for the birthday party with our car stuck?! Could our day get ANY worse?

We had to see for ourselves. Mind swung the corner of the curtain up ...

Yup. Our day just got a whole LOT worse.

Forget about trying not to see ONE

Rao. Today there were FOUR Rao's on our doorstep: Sara Rao, her parents Mr and Mrs Rao, plus . . . BABY RAO?!

'I invited them over,' Mama walked past us with a duster.

'You did WHAT?!' Papa and I both froze.

'Friendship is the glue that holds a team together. If you can't get along, your team won't be as strong!'

Mama dusted a cobweb off the ceiling and then fluffed the cushions on the sofa, the way she always does when we've got company.

'All set!' she admired her work.

Knock-knock! We heard at the front door.

'Perfect timing,' she sailed by to welcome the guests in. 'Ahhh, come in, come in!'

Baby Rao grabbed at strands of Mama's hair to play with, drooling happily.

'Sorry, he's teething and likes to put

everything straight into his mouth!' Mrs Rao apologised and tickled the baby's hand off Mama.

'Awww he's adorable! Reminds me of when Maya was a baby! Maya, why don't you show Sara your Pooey?'

Sara looked horrified and Mind had turned redder than the roses in the bouquet Mrs Rao had brought us.

'Pooey is my pet rabbit.'
I led Sara through the house and into the back garden.

By the time we got there, Papa and Mr Rao were already through the side gate and at the veggie patch, discussing all things carroty.

'The truth is, if you win on biggest roots, you lose out on best flavour . . .' Mr Rao's head bobbed up and down as he talked to Papa, who was concentrating on every word he said and jotting down notes.

'If you keep planting seeds, you can get fresh carrots all year long, so we enjoy eating them in the Spring while they're sweet and crunchy ... We love to boil and blend them into a mash for the little one!'

'Uh-huh,' Papa nodded enthusiastically.

'Then, I get down to the serious business of competition carrots!'

That was when I saw something I thought I'd *never* see: Papa fist-bumping Mr Rao.

'May the best carrots win!'

If *they* of all people could share some common ground (even if it was only over a veggie patch) surely Sara and I could be friendly too ...

'I helped my Papa to plant some carrots yesterday . . .' I started, a bit nervous about what to say. 'Pooey, my pet rabbit, loves carrots.'

'I didn't know you had a pet rabbit,' Sara replied, shyer than I expected her to be.

'I didn't know you had a baby brother!' I felt my cheeks turn red as soon as I spoke.

Oiii! You can't compare their baby to your pet! Mind pointed out, a bit late.

But it made Sara laugh and say something funny back: 'Well, my baby brother could be called Pooey too. He has a *lot* of pooey nappies!'

I could just about remember the last time I ever giggled about poo talk. It was probably back when I was still a Bub and didn't know or care about the R.E.A.L. rules. It made Mind feel playful.

'Do you want to play?'

'Sure, as long as it's not a sport. I play sports all week long, so I like to chill on the weekend and take a break from games like that.'

Well, I never! Mind was flabbergasted. *Superstar Sara doesn't like SPORTS?!*

I figured Sara liked sports but that everyone needs a break sometimes, even from the things we like. Even sports superstars.

And especially from the things we don't like! Mind hid behind a tree. Mega-Coach Mama was heading over with my cricket gear in hand.

'Right, girls . . .' she handed me the ball. 'You can use the patio as a pitch and I'll mark the boundary in the grass just like the edge of a real cricket field, for you to practice your game.'

Speaking of *boundaries,* I wished more than anything that I could mark out a boundary of my own to keep Mega-Coach

Mama away. Only *my* Mama would be allowed to cross that boundary.

'Mamaaa . . .' Papa came over and took the ball off me. 'We had *other* plans for the girls this morning, *remember . . .?*'

Mama put the stumps back inside their cover, like she had been caught doing something she knew she shouldn't.

'Follow me,' Papa beckoned.

He had set up the kitchen table with the messy tablecloth out and lots of little pots of colours, shape cutters and decorations to choose from. It was almost how it looked when we did arts and crafts. But not quite. I could tell Sara was as excited as Mind and me, because she reached for a brush at the same time as us.

Where's the paper? Mind looked up.

That's when we saw Papa carrying over a TRAY full of . . . CUPCAKES!

'Now, ALL of these are for you two to decorate however you like. Except for this one!' Papa popped a whole cupcake straight into his mouth.

'As long as you both remember . . .' he tried to use his strict voice to get our attention, but cupcake crumbs kept falling out of his mouth, distracting Mind. Papa shook some of the sprinkles out of the jar and into his hand. 'You must clean your hands after!' He stuck his tongue out and licked all the sprinkles off his palm, munching on them with a silly smile on his face.

Sara and I got stuck in, giggling and drizzling icing all over our cupcakes (and ourselves!).

Best way to get rid of the extra icing . . . ? Mind gave my fingers a lick clean. **SLURP!**

We didn't need telling THRICE.

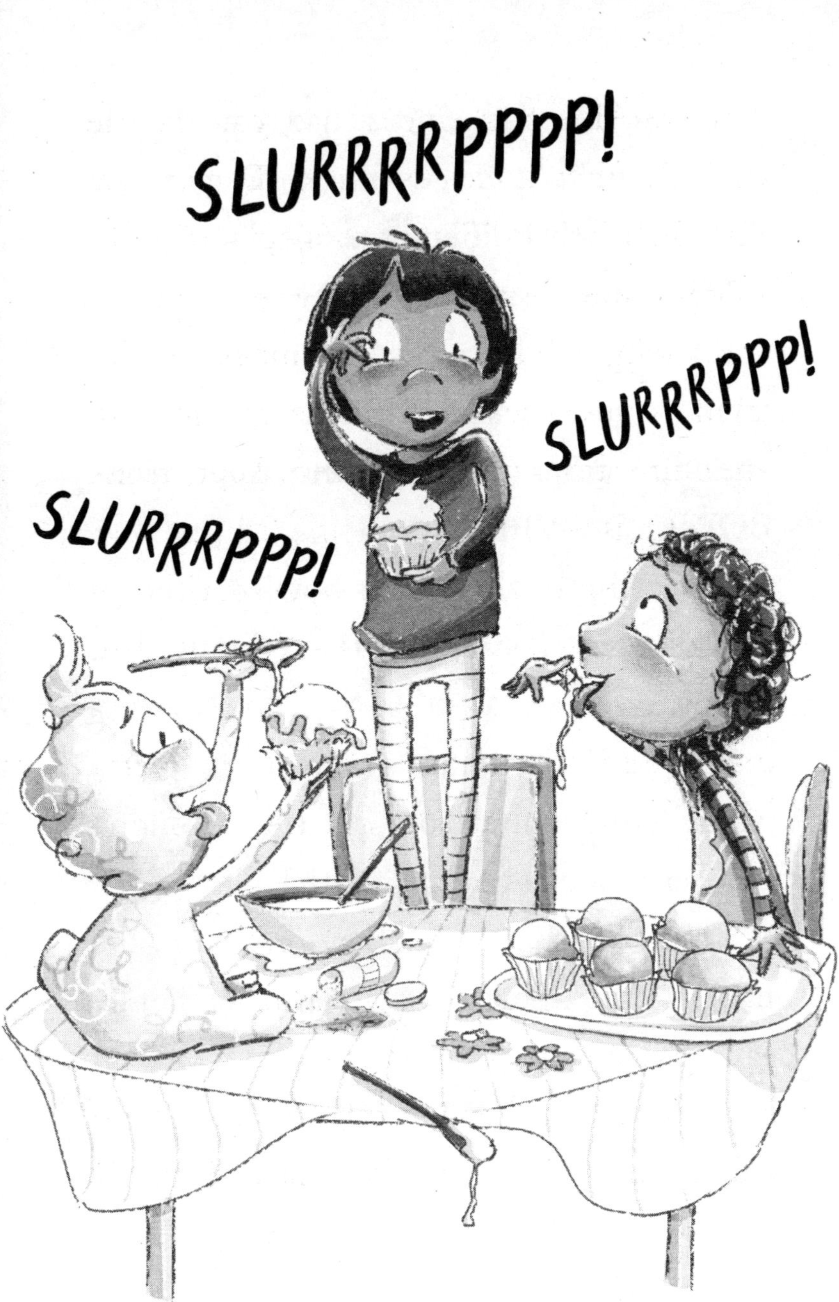
SLURRRRPPPP!
SLURRRPPP!
SLURRRPPP!

It was like Sara and I had exactly the same thought at exactly the same moment. We weren't that different at all!

Mind was as surprised as I was.

If a hat-trick in cricket meant the bowler taking three wickets with three balls, one after the other . . . we were three times BOWLED OVER!!!

First: Mind and I were bowled over by the discovery that the Rao family had a baby.

Second: That gift, wrapped in pretty paper with a shiny bow on it – I couldn't believe Sara had got me a GIFT.

Third: This was a big one, for the hat-trick . . . Seeing Sara with her family at home, I didn't see *Sara* as the show-off *Superstar* . . . instead I saw her as someone's daughter, a sister, and now my friend – or *saheli* as Mama would say in Hindi.

Superstar Sara had become *Saheli Sara*!

'Time to go!' Papa slipped his arm into one sleeve of his jacket.

Go where? Mind looked up.

We were having such a fun time with Sara decorating cupcakes that we'd almost forgotten it was time to go to Tanya and Anya's birthday party!

'Ooh, Sara, this gift looks lovely . . .' Mama pointed to it, but didn't pick it up or pass it to me. 'I'm sure Tanya and Anya will love it!'

Mind wiped the smile off my face and frowned, taking a bite out of a cupcake.

If the gift wasn't for us after all, we were at least going to have our share of cupcakes

. . . before someone told us they weren't for us either!

As everyone got ready to head out, Mind braced me for another afternoon of watching Tanya winning. Bowling wasn't my thing, like so many things, and Captain Tanya's birthday bowling was bound to be brilliant.

What exactly is our THING? Mind wondered, picking up some cake crumbs as we got into the car.

Making memories was something we were extremely good at! Except now we spent ALL our time practising for Cricket Club, instead of doing anything special together to make new memories.

Mind went blank.

There wasn't single thing we could think of that was *our thing*.

We had . . .

'Ohhhhhhhhh!' I wailed out so loud that Mama almost lost control of the steering wheel and swerved us off the road.

She stopped the car safely and checked if I was okay.

'*Kya hua*, Maya?' she asked, turning around to look at me from the driver's seat.

It felt like the first time in a very, *very*, VERY long time she was actually taking the time to look at me in my eyes. She had stopped everything she was doing to talk to me. It was just us two together, with no one else around and no distractions. This was our moment. So I took it!

'Everything's going wrong!' I cried.

'What do you mean?'

'I wish we'd never made a Cricket Club.'

We both went quiet. She switched off the car engine and clicked her seatbelt off. She turned herself around even more to face me and leaned over to hold my hand.

'It's okay.' She stroked the back of my hand gently with her thumb. 'It isn't always easy to tell each other how we feel, so thank you for telling me.'

Mama made Mind and me want to open up even more and let it all out.

'There's no time for anything else now that we do Cricket Club. I can't get Mama-and-Maya time anymore, I can't write my letter to Grandpa by myself, I can't play with Pooey because I'm too tired from playing cricket all the time, and worst of all ... I can't even play cricket all that well!'

'Oh, Maya,' Mama smiled softly and put her hand on my cheek. 'You're right. We have been too busy. You don't have to play cricket anymore if you're not happy.'

Really?! Mind couldn't believe what we were hearing.

'You don't mind if I don't play cricket? I thought Cricket Club meant the world to you.'

Mind took the black and white photo out and passed it to me to show Mama.

Mama took a long look at it.

'Maya, the only thing that matters to me, more than anything else in the whole world . . . is that you are okay. I'm really sorry I've gone a bit more *cricket-y* than I probably should have. I loved cricket when I was little, but that doesn't mean you have to.'

'It's all right, Mama. I know it's important to you. I don't mind, as long as we can still do other things together.'

'Doing what *you* want to do together is what's important to me.' She gave my hand a little squeeze. 'I tell you what . . . Let's enjoy this party today and forget all about cricket for now, eh?'

I sniffled a couple of times, before realising I still hadn't asked Mama about what was worrying me.

'Is there anything else on your mind? You can ask me anything you like. That's what I'm here for . . .'

Mind flicked through a notepad full of questions we'd been saving up to go through with Mama.

'What does *Krankenhaus* mean?'

Mama looked surprised at first, then calmly explained, '*Krankenhaus* means hospital, in German. Grandpa has been to hospital a couple of times this year because he was poorly and he couldn't remember things very well. As we get older, sometimes it can get harder to look after ourselves. So that's why he needed some help at home. He is doing better now but his memory isn't as strong as it used to be.'

'Is he going to be okay?'

'Yes, he is being looked after really well

by doctors and nurses who care for older people who live alone. But we're thinking of having him stay here with us for a while. How do you feel about that?'

Wowww! Imagine if Grandpa came to visit . . . Mind couldn't have been happier to know that we might get to see Grandpa again soon and started imagining all sorts of things we could do together. When Grandpa got to our house, we'd take him upstairs to show him the rainbow wall in my room, then we'd take Pooey out of her hutch to give him some *khargoshi* cuddles (that *always* cheered me up when I was unwell) . . .

AND . . . We could take Grandpa along to our next big Cricket Club match. That would be super fun! Mind beamed.

'I'd love to see Grandpa again! And I do want to stick at Cricket Club!'

'If that's what *you* want to do, I'm here to help. Just remember, it's meant to be fun.'

I nodded.

'I'll try to remember that too,' Mama winked. 'Let's do it, TEAM!'

This time, when Mama said 'team', it felt like she meant *me and her:* my favourite team of all.

Mama let go of my hand and reached for her seatbelt. 'Now, any other questions before we get on our way to this party?'

'Err . . . just one . . .' I couldn't let it go. 'What's a jaffa?!'

Mama laughed –

'It's just a word for a type of bowling that gets a batter out, or comes very close to getting them out. We can forget about all of that for now and go have some FUN!'

That was the BEST thing Mama could have said to me and Mind. It was just what we needed to hear. Cricket definitely wasn't the most important thing to her . . . WE were!

Tanya won every frame of the game at her and Anya's bowling birthday bash, just as we thought she would, but Mind and me still had a blast at the party with all our friends. Tanya was the best bowler in every sport she played. But, this was the break from cricket practice we'd needed.

Being away from cricket for a while and having fun with our friends, rather than spending all our time together as a team training for a tournament, had got us feeling quite excited about getting back into it at the big game tomorrow. If we kept playing cricket, by the time Grandpa came to visit, we'd be so confident!

That night, as Mama tucked Mind and me into bed, I felt a rush of energy run through me like electricity through a wire and Mind lit up like a lamp. It was our last sleep before the BIG GAME and Mind had a brilliant IDEA!

Sure, I couldn't be the Captain of the team, or even *the* Vice Captain (because technically I was CO-Vice Captain) but that didn't mean I *couldn't* be the BEST

Co-Vice Captain EVER. All I had to do was work super well together with my *Saheli* Sara to back our Captain Tanya, and lead our team to victory. Imagine the celebration if we won ... And the bottom line was that we wanted to win. So Mind was, for now at least, totally on board with the idea!

Mind was glowing, and not just like any light but like the flame of a small clay lamp called a *diya*. I blinked my eyes and Mind flickered like something from the past ...

Another MEMORY MOMENT! There were colourful, painted *diyas* everywhere, glistening in pretty patterns outside all the doors and in rows sparkling along every windowsill, inviting in the gods for luck. It was Diwali time, the Festival of Lights in India. We were back at Grandpa's house, standing on the balcony and watching fireworks across the city skyline, bursting like bright rainbow fireballs and decorating the night!

We remembered Grandpa's words and his voice swirled around us:

'*Diwali* is a celebration of the greatest victory of all ... The power of light winning over darkness!'

Mind glowed warm and bright all through the night, full of hope for tomorrow and lighting a path for us to get to our dreams.

CHAPTER 11

GOOOOOD MORNINGGGGGG . . . SPORTSDAY FANS!!! It's the moment we've all been waiting for . . .

The commentator's voice boomed out of the speakers into the audience. It was Mr Drodge, our Headteacher, sitting next to the Headteacher of Sunnydale School, Mrs Sharma. We were about to make our grand entrance.

Heeere they come! It's the Shooting Stars!

Tanya, Captain of our team, walked out onto the school field first, followed by Sara, our Co-Vice Captain, and then Mind and me. I was so nervous at this point,

I was almost glad not to be right at the front. I didn't care if anyone knew I was Co-Vice Captain or not! Mind, on the other hand, was loving the attention. Mind waved at the rows full of families and friends sitting on the edge of their seats — parents, brothers, sisters, aunts, uncles, cousins, grandparents (and even some pets!) were there to show their support. They clapped fiercely as the commentators welcomed the two school cricket teams out, almost as if it was a competition between the loudest claps.

If only! Mind liked the idea of skipping the game and walking off as winners right now. It was obvious to Mind that *our* well-wishers were by far the loudest. Aunty Dolly held up the biggest banner, and waved it at us while singing out a cheer for everyone to hear:

Captain Tanya's the only LASS
Who's got the right kind of SASS
To get our team out on the GRASS
And show 'em all our game's TOP CLASS!

Anya's the best team mate AROUND
Winning or losing, she'll never FROWN
She's got the best game-face in TOWN
So, bring it on – she's always DOWN!

Maya the Flyer's on her WAY
She's Cap'n Tanya's wing-girl TODAY
Maya's sharing the job, WAH-HAY
We wouldn't have it any other WAY!

I could always rely on Aunty Dolly to make me smile.

The perfect rhyme, right on time! Mind winked at her and then blew kisses to the crowd. Mind looked like a rock star going on stage, ready to perform a set of greatest hits to our adoring fans! To Mind, Co-Vice Captain was one of the TOP 2 players in a team of eleven, right after Captain. That was IMPRESSIVE stuff!

Aunty Dolly waved and then tripped, falling into Papa, her banner nearly whacking him in the face. He ducked down and got out of the way, but he'd moved too fast for the scoops of ice cream in his cup to keep up . . . three big blobs of ice cream (what looked like vanilla, strawberry and chocolate) caught Mr Rao's sun hat and went splat, *splat,* and *SPLAT* all over it, like bird poop.

Talk about a hat-trick! Mind chuckled, but then ditched me to catch up with our Co-Vice Captain Sara. There was no way Mind was going to let her get all the glory, walking beside Captain Tanya, with us left trailing behind.

I rolled my eyes. I wasn't bothered about all that anymore. There were much bigger things at stake here – like people's FEELINGS. Every single one of our team members mattered. Without them all, we had no team. But Mind smirked at me and then got straight back to practising signing autographs to give everyone after our win. I had no idea why Mind was showing off so much, or how Mind was so confident about us winning, even before the game had started.

Let the games BEGIN!

Folks, what you're about to witness is no ordinary toss of a coin ... It's CRUNCH TIME!

The side that wins this COIN TOSS decides whether to bat or bowl first. It's the first and possibly biggest decision of the match for these two Team Captains – Captain Tanya versus Captain Kemi.

Get it wrong, and risk taking your team down a path to defeat.

Get it RIGHT, and you might just have the match trophy coming your way!

Mind couldn't help notice Captain Kemi was extremely neat, with sports clothes that were sparkling clean and ironed, her hair in the tidiest of braids, tied back and away from her face – unlike Tanya, whose ponytails were as messy as ever, with bits of fringe in her eyes, and mud-stained clothes that looked like they hadn't been washed since the rainy day we caught the train to the batting nets. It made Mind look at me and the rest of our team with some *doubt* about how presentable any of us looked. Even our fans weren't the best dressed . . .

We glanced over at the audience. Papa, in his old flip flops he'd taped back together when the strap broke, and Mr Rao, with ice cream melting down his hat now, were sharing a pot of carrot sticks and laughing. That made Mind really stop and stare. It was unbelievable that Mr Rao, Papa's arch rival a few weeks ago as far as carrot competitions go, had become such good friends that they wanted to grow and eat carrots together, instead of trying to outgrow and beat each other's carrots.

Never judge a book by its cover – never judge a player by their looks!

Yet another one of Mama's coaching catchphrases came back to us in that moment. Her wise words were proving to be spot on. It was as though she and Papa had been planting seeds for Mind and me the whole time. Now the sweetest and crunchiest carrots were cropping from those seeds right on time, when we needed them most.

It didn't matter what we looked like on the outside, it was what we had on the inside that counted! Our team and our fans had *heart*. We *stuck together*.

Mind whispered: *Heart is good, but back to the coin toss . . . Heads or Tails? I say, Heads, we win . . . Tails, we lose!*

WHY would Mind say that?!

Sure, we knew that we needed our heads

to win . . . but what if the coin landed Tails up now? We'd be going into the game with the feeling that we were bound to lose.

'What do you think?' Tanya asked Sara and me. 'Should we go for Heads or—'

'Heads!' I butted in, since Mind was set.

The umpire flipped the coin and it spun high up in the air like a trapeze artist at the circus, catching the sun and glinting at us before landing back on the palm of his hand to reveal . . .

Heads . . . YESSS!!! Mind was overjoyed, but didn't realise that winning the toss wasn't the same as winning the game.

'We'll *bowl* first,' Captain Tanya confirmed and shook the umpire's hand. We knew she would choose to bowl first. Being such a strong bowler meant that Tanya could stop the opposite team getting too high a score if they batted first and really set us up for a good innings after that.

There you have it, everyone ...

The home team, Shooting Stars, WIN the toss and have chosen to BOWL first! Not what I would have done, but there you have it! Captain Tanya leading the way, HER WAY ...

Mind wondered what Mr Drodge meant by that. What would *he* have done? Maybe the pitch was dry and dusty so he thought batting first was better?? Maybe the other team's bowling was stronger than ours???

Tanya didn't seem to pay any mind to what was being said but what if she had got it wrong?!

This time, one of Papa's pearls of wisdom reminded us to focus on ourselves, do what we had to do, and not let anything or anyone throw us off course: *A carrot doesn't look at the carrot next to it. It just keeps growing. So you just keep going!*

Looking over at Papa for reassurance, we saw him jumping up and down with both thumbs up at us. That gave us the go ahead to just keep going!

Out on the playing field, Captain Tanya checked all of us were in position to *field* (that meant catching the ball once the batter hits it, to get them OUT!).

Then she did her run up to bowl the first ball of the game.

Let's hope Captain Tanya starts as she means to go on . . .

The fastest bowler on our side, Tanya whizzed down the field, right up to the pitch, and flung the ball at top speed towards the wicket. Captain Kemi, starting the batting for their side, galloped towards the ball, with no hesitation and struck the ball HARD.

That one's gone into orbit!

The umpire's signalling a SIX, so a six it is, to start the innings! Captain Kemi is officially off the mark and in STYLE! What a start for the Sixer Strikers . . .

Mind fell silent. We could only hope that Tanya hadn't started as she meant to go on . . .

Buddy Beth, wicket-keeping for our team, walked down the pitch to give Tanya a pat on the back and some words we couldn't hear from where I was standing, further out in the field.

Tanya prepared for another run up. Mind and me bent forward slightly, hands on our knees, ready and waiting to catch the next ball.

THWACK!!!

The ball landed in a gap between our fielders and rolled like a bowling ball all the way to the boundary.

Clipped away for four!

The umpire ran her hand across to gesture a FOUR. Mind was starting to flap – what had happened to Tanya, the best bowler in every sport we knew?!

TEN runs in just TWO balls . . . Captain Kemi is on TOP FORM.

Captain Kemi and her teammate

celebrated her shots with a hug. She pointed her bat up at the sky, as if they were chatting about something easy-breezy like the weather. This was a BREEZE for them! Tanya really needed to UP her game, before *they* upped their score out of our reach!

Both players walked back to their places at either end of the pitch and Captain Kemi fixed her helmet, forcing Tanya to wait until she was ready for the next ball. I could tell Tanya was getting impatient. So was Mind!

Mind pointed furiously to an imaginary wrist-watch and pretended to check the time, as if to say: *Stop stalling!*

There was nothing anyone could do about it. Not even *the umpire*. It was like a POWER move by Captain Kemi, to show everyone who was *really* in charge of this game.

If they carry on like this, these two bold batters are going to rack up a very high score indeed for the Sixer Strikers. I wouldn't want to be chasing that!

But that was exactly what we faced chasing, as our team's turn to bat was only a few more balls away. If we didn't start doing something *very* differently, *very* soon, we'd be chasing a *very* high score *indeed*, as Mr Drodge put it!

CHAPTER 12

TOOOOOOOOOOOOOT!

Mr Drodge blew the whistle.

Whew! Finally, break time. Mind couldn't have been more relieved.

It was the end of the Sixer Strikers' innings. Our turn to bowl had gone by in a flash! And our turn to bat was about to begin. We had to turn things around after the break.

We needed to change our game plan and the only way to do that was with . . . a Team Talk. The other team's turn to bat was already over! And ours would be over just as quick. Coach Mama was right —

T2 cricket really was the speediest game anyone had ever seen. If we weren't careful, we were about to see the shortest game of T2 cricket ever ... If we batted as badly as we had bowled, we'd be ALL OUT before we got anywhere near the whopping 34 runs Captain Kemi's team had scored. The Sixer Strikers had lived up to their name, striking almost every ball for six!

Walking past the crowd as we left the field, I couldn't see Papa anywhere. Surely he hadn't left half way through the game?!

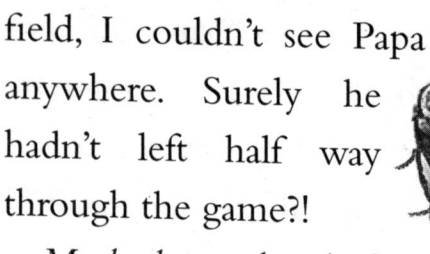

Maybe he got bored of watching us losing ...

Mind wasn't feeling very hopeful anymore. I just about managed to drag us back into the changing rooms for the break. We were the last ones in. Our entire team was sitting silently. We could tell something was up. We'd obviously missed something big.

'We're not going back out there.' Beth crossed her arms. 'Not with Tanya as Captain anyway.'

'Why, what happened? Where *is* Tanya?!'

'Why don't you ask *her* . . . she's *your* cousin, after all!' someone called out.

Nobody moved. It was like my nightmare, except instead of my bat being glued to the ground, it was as if everyone's bums had been glued to the benches.

Friendship is the glue that holds a team together. If you can't get along, your team won't be as strong! Coach Mama's words came back to Mind. Where was Mama, anyway?

We had no chance of coming up with a new game plan, without our Coach or Captain!

'Tanya went *that* way . . .' Sara pointed to the toilets.

That's where I found Anya, crouched down on the floor, next to Tanya who was leaning against a sink with her hands over her face.

'Are you okay?' I wasn't used to seeing Tanya down-hearted. She was always full of energy.

'Well . . .' Anya began to explain. 'Some of the team said they weren't very happy with how the game was going . . .'

'You mean, they tried to BLAME me and my bowling,' Tanya's muffled voice interjected through her fingers.

'Yes,' Anya went on. ' . . . and that was when Tanya decided to remind everyone how she bowled better than any of them at our birthday party yesterday and that she is the best player on our team, so she should lead the batting after the break.'

'Oh.'

Suddenly it made sense that the team were upset.

'They said Tanya shouldn't open the batting and she should give someone else a turn to lead.'

'You mean, they tried to overrule me . . . their Captain!'

'So . . .' Anya tried to finish. '. . . that's when Tanya told everyone she's the Captain, which makes her the BOSS and what she says, goes!'

To Mind and me, it sounded like Tanya's bossiness had got the better of her. No one liked being bossed around. We knew that from all the times Tanya had bossed *us* about. But we also knew Tanya couldn't help being bossy sometimes and that she meant well (most of the time).

'We know you're trying your best,' I put my hand on Tanya's shoulder and then made a suggestion. 'It might be helpful to let other people in the team have a say too, so they feel like you care about what they think.'

Tanya finally looked up. Her eyes were pink and teary.

'Team-work makes the dream work,' I grinned at her.

Mind couldn't believe just how handy Coach Mama's funny phrases had turned out to be!

'Thanks, Maya. I *know* I'm the best Captain for our team. I just need a chance to *show* them.'

Tanya always believed in herself. Even when people around her didn't. That's what we needed now. Everyone thought our team was about to lose, and the only thing that might get us back out onto that field was to believe in ourselves. We could still win if we believed it.

Let's go talk to the team. We've got to remind them why they voted for Tanya to be our Captain in the first place.

'I'll be right back,' I pushed the door open to the changing rooms again. This time everyone was up on their feet and looked like they'd been talking about something.

'I vote for MAYA, our Co-Vice Captain to take over as CAPTAIN of the team!' Beth jumped up onto a bench and declared, with both arms up in the air.

'Hooooo-raaaaayyy!' some others joined her and clapped for me.

YESSS!!! Mind's eyes lit up. It seemed like Mind loved the IDEA of being a winner so much that it was all Mind could think about. Mind was convinced that this was our moment to shine and that we'd better make the most of it while it lasted. To Mind, we were *cooler* than the Cools right now.

I didn't feel the same way at all.

Besides, had Mind forgotten what we'd just said to Tanya and Anya?! I needed to talk to Mind for a moment.

'Just give me a sec . . .' I headed outside.

'Sure, *Captain!* We're right here and ready to follow your lead.'

How was I going to get Mind to see my point of view? I took a deep breath, looked up at the bright sky, trying not to look straight at the sun and then I looked all the way back down to the grass growing on the muddy ground.

Mind, look at that!

This grass, just like Papa's carrot patch, grows its best when the sun brings the light, the rain brings the water, the earth brings the soil. Everything has its own important part to play. We both know Tanya is the best cricket player here. She's the right person to play the part of Captain. She's having a rough time. It's *our* part to play, as Co-Vice Captain, to support her and help the rest of the team to play our best together. *That* is how *we* shine. So let's be the best Co-Vice Captain we can be!

An empty plastic bottle blowing in the wind clattered past and over to the audience. Papa was back! This time, he had Pooey with him. So *that* was where he'd gone earlier – he'd been home to get her so she could watch me play.

He held her up in the air and waved her furry paws at us, while Aunty Dolly stroked the soft spot between her ears, just the way she liked it. Tanya and Anya's Dad wasn't at their Sports Day. He wasn't around much of the time at all. I wondered how that might feel. There were lots of things I didn't fully understand about grown-ups . . . like Grandpa's health. And there are plenty of things about the world that don't make much sense. Like that

piece of rubbish that someone threw outside, littering on Planet Earth, instead of just putting it in a recycling bin. But what I *did* understand was how it felt when someone was kind to me, when I needed some kindness. It was the best gift I could imagine and the greatest kind of WIN for everyone.

This was our moment to SHINE. Light over darkness . . . kindness over unkindness!

It was so clear to me. It didn't need another moment's thought. I clutched onto Mind and hopped right back in to the changing rooms.

'Right, team! Let's show our Captain some support!'

'Give over!' someone heckled. 'You're just saying that because Tanya's your cousin!'

'Exactly!' someone else jeered in agreement.

'If *you* can't step up, Maya, one of *us* will!'

We're losing them ... Mind pulled me aside ... *and if we lose the team, we lose the game!*

Mind had a point. But what was I supposed to do? They weren't listening to me even though I was Co-Vice Captain! It felt like I was drifting into the deep end of a swimming pool. I needed help!

You're not the only Co-Vice Captain around here! Mind objected.

What a time to bring that up! Mind knew how disappointed I'd felt about having to share the job with *Superstar Sara* ... I wondered whose side Mind was on?!

Mind nudged me and nodded in the direction of Sara.

What I mean is that your Co-Vice Captain is not your cousin! She's not Tanya's cousin either, so the others might listen to her, if they won't listen to you!

Mind threw some more words my way. Finally, I got what Mind meant and it was like a float I could cling on to and bob back to safety with.

I had to get Sara on side. If *she* could convince the team that Tanya was the best Captain for us, we'd be back in the game!

'If you don't believe me, ask Sara, she's Vice Captain too . . .' I looked over to my friend, *Saheli Sara,* for her help. 'Tanya might be BOSSY but she's also *SASSY!* That's what got us as far as we've come in this game. Without Tanya's SASS, we've got no chance!'

'That's right.' *Saheli* Sara stepped up to stand with me, like a true friend. 'I'm with Maya.'

'Me too!' Beth stood next to us.

'Me three!' Anya showed up just in time, along with Tanya.

'WE CAN DO THIS, TEAM!' Tanya skipped through and climbed up onto a bench in the middle of the room. All eyes were on her now.

'You *really* still believe we can win this?'

'I believe in *you* . . .' Tanya nodded at each and every member of our team. ' . . . and you, and you, and you! I believe in US!'

'You're the only one!

'And *that* is why *I* am your Captain!' Tanya sounded more confident than ever.

'Let's get back out there! We've got to be in it to WIN IT.'

Mind wasn't sure about winning the game, but Tanya was definitely winning back her team.

'She's right, everyone – this is *not* the time for falling out,' Sara backed her Captain and that made everyone else want to back her too. Everyone had gathered around us in a circle now.

'Team work makes the dream work!' Tanya winked at me and handed me my gloves and helmet. 'Maya and Sara will open the batting for us.'

'That's more like it!' someone high fived Tanya.

'Yeaaah! Go Captain Tanya!'

I was glad the team was getting along again. But how did anyone expect *me* to open the batting for us?

If only we had Grandpa's lucky bat! Mind sighed.

BOOM!!

Mama slammed the door open and lunged forwards into the room. She had brought a bat for me and started to unzip the cover – just in time too! But Mind sensed straight away that this wasn't just any bat. Mind was right . . . It was the bat of our dreams!

'Grandpa's bat!' Mama panted, out of breath, as she presented our lucky bat to us. My heart jumped like a fielder on the pitch, taking a winning catch.

'Where did you find it?!' I gasped, giving Mama and the bat a big hug.

'Well, Papa nipped home to get Pooey so she could watch you bat. And when I saw her hopping around the cricket field, I suddenly remembered . . . we'd kept Grandpa's bat in your room, right behind Pooey's hutch. So, I *had* to dash home and get it for you. I know how much it means to you, Maya.'

Sweat ran down the side of Mama's face, as she knelt down and handed the bat over to me. For a second, she looked like that little girl again in the black and white picture, just like Mind and me –

GOING TO BAT.
TOOOOOOOOOOOOOT!!!
We heard the whistle from outside for the start of play again.

'We're the *Shooting Stars* and we're going to *shoot* for the *stars!*' Tanya wafted her hands up above us, like stars shooting across the sky. She jumped off the bench and started a cheer to lead the team back onto the field:

'Shooting Stars!
Shooting STARS!
They can't stop us,
This game's OURS!'

One by one, each of the *Shooting Stars* followed her out, except for Sara and me. We hung back to get kitted up and ready to bat. It felt almost unreal to Mind and me . . . Just over a week ago we'd started a Cricket Club and now we were at our school's Sports Day, standing at the bowling end of the pitch, waiting and watching as the bowler ran in to bowl the first ball to *Saheli* Sara.

The ball zoomed past and straight into the wickets behind Sara's bat. As real as real can be, the bails flew off and their whole team, all of the Sixer Strikers, yelled –

HOWZAAAAAAT!!!

The umpire's finger went straight up in the air.

Unbelievable ... out for a duck!

Like Mr Drodge, Mind was shocked. Sara was one of our strongest players. Now she was OUT with ZERO runs – a DUCK!

'Quack!'
'Quack!'
'Quack!'
'Quack!'

The other team's fielders called out as Sara walked off, and Anya took to the batting crease.

That riled Mind. We were sticking to the rules and the visiting team on *our* turf, at *our* school, were breaking all the rules with unkind words towards *our* team!

Mind was more determined than ever now, to turn the angry feeling inside, into a winning feeling out on the pitch.

Anya was no sports superstar but she was someone we could count on to keep her wicket safe and give us a chance to score. Anya managed a single run, which got Mind and me on strike and facing our first ball.

With Grandpa's lucky bat in our hands, Mind felt like we had all the luck in the world on our side.

Mind swung the bat hard and drove the

ball all the way to the boundary, with all the power of England's team of lions and India's tigers, roaring WELL DONE to ourselves: *SHABASH!*

She's off the mark! Maya gets the innings off to a strong start with a FOUR for the Shooting Stars. Could this be the game-changing shot they needed . . . ?

My shot and the first four for our team on the scoreboard . . . Mind was fired up! But, one by one, the other batters on our team were bowled or caught out, until we were almost ALL OUT.

The Sixer Strikers were close to winning the game and they knew it.

It threw me and I missed my shot.

'Try bowling her a piano . . . See if she can play that!' the wicket-keeper joked.

When our last batter, Tara, one of the Bubs, walked out to join me, the bowler laughed. 'Ohhh . . . a Bub with a bat!'

'They're distracting our players!' Tanya huffed.

'I'm about to knock those wickets over with this next ball, like knocking out your milk teeth, Bub!'

That's breaking the rules! Those were definitely NOT kind words . . . Mind was disgusted.

There was only one ball left until the end of the game and we needed six more runs to win. I had to hit this higher and further than I'd ever hit a cricket ball.

'Don't let them get to you, Maya . . .' Tanya yelled from the side lines. 'You've got this . . .'

Tanya had always shown me how to stick up for myself. It was time to use everything we'd ever learnt.

I squinted my eyes at Captain Kemi under the shade of the peak of my helmet and then pulled my lip and nostril up at her, chin and cheek crumpling up into a full-on snarl. Not just any snarl. This one was for the trophy: the Sports Day SUPER SNARL!

It's not over, until the OVER is over!

Mr Drodge's voice blared out of the speakers, reminding us all the game wasn't over yet. *One ball to go . . .*

'Lift, Maya, lift!' Coach Mama's voice echoed in my ears.

Mind focused in on what Mama had meant . . . Years ago, Grandpa had shown me how to lift my bat even when it felt too heavy. Mind slid my hand a teeny-weeny bit further down the handle of my bat to just the right spot. *That* was where we found what we had been looking for – the missing piece of the puzzle!

All our MEMORY MOMENTS came together, and I whacked the ball high up into the sky like Pooey on my space-hopper and all the way out of the school playing fields. We looked over at the Umpire, who lifted both arms straight up into the air.

It was a SIX!!!!!! Mind knew what that meant . . .

They've done it! They've WON it!

It was official. Mind and me, we could hardly believe it.

What a way to end the game . . . truly remarkable scenes here at our first ever Sports Day cricket match! Maya and the Shooting Stars have won the game, against the odds!

Our team ran out onto the field. Tanya tooted Miss Wong's whistle, while Buddy Beth gave everyone piggybacks around the pitch, *Saheli* Sara somersaulted, and Anya's arms up in the air made her look like she was on a rollercoaster ride.

Each one of us was *different* in so many ways but we'd come together to do something that made us feel the *same* — winning the game! We couldn't have done any of it without each other. We had learnt a lot about ourselves, each other, and cricket of course!

I'd just hit my very first SIX to win us the game!

Papa passed Pooey to me, along with a carrot she was nibbling on. Mr Rao came over too.

'Well done, Maya!' Sara gave me a hug with one arm. 'Pooey is going to love the carrots you planted with those green fingers of yours!'

Mind's eyes shot straight to my hands,

which were thankfully not green at all but just their normal skin colour.

'Green fingers – it's just a way of saying you're great at growing plants!' Mr Rao chuckled.

Imagine how far we'd all come: Sara wasn't just a Sportstar to me anymore but my *Saheli*! Beth had gone from Bully to Buddy! And Mind was more interested in turning our *green fingers* to gardening, than worrying about jealous feelings turning us into an imaginary green monster!

We were so busy celebrating together, the actual prize we'd won was the last thing on our minds.

'I need my two Co-Vice Captains!' Captain Tanya called me and Sara over to help lift up the heavy trophy for a team photograph.

Don't forget, Grandpa's bat! Mind made

sure I was holding our lucky bat, so we could send the photo to Grandpa, like we'd dreamed of weeks ago, before we started the Cricket Club.

All our dreams are coming true! Nightmares, go away now – shoo! Mind cheered us on.

When it was all over and we got home, we finally had some time just for us. At last, it was just Mama (not Coach

Mama), Papa, Pooey and me.

FAMILY TIME!!! For Mind and me, *that* was the best prize of all.

The only one missing was Grandpa . . .

Not for long, if he's coming to stay, like Mama said! Mind dug an elbow into my side.

The last few weeks had brought back so many old memories of being together with Grandpa in India. We were looking forward to making lots of new memories when Grandpa got here. I couldn't wait to finish my letter to Grandpa now; I had so much to tell him and knew he'd love to hear all about our big game!

With a pen in my hand and Mama by my side, ready to help with the Hindi words, I opened the envelope and found the letter I'd started writing all those weeks ago. That was when Mind had asked the question about when we had last written to Grandpa.

But HERE and NOW, in this moment, there was only *one* question that mattered to Mind and me, that we needed to ask more than anything:

Dear Grandpa,

When are you coming to stay?!

DEDICATION

To Gaurav, my star.
Everything I do is for you, Shreya and Aarav.
Family trees are forever.

To my grandparents, Asha & Ganesh and Raj Rani
& Murari Lal, for all our memory moments.

To my parents, Rohini & Rajiv, for helping me
solve life's puzzles.

To Satya & Satish for cheering for me.

To my brothers, sisters, family and friends (you know
who you are!) – the best team I could ever wish for.

To Avani & Jovan, Leela & Nikhil, Roman & Keirsson.

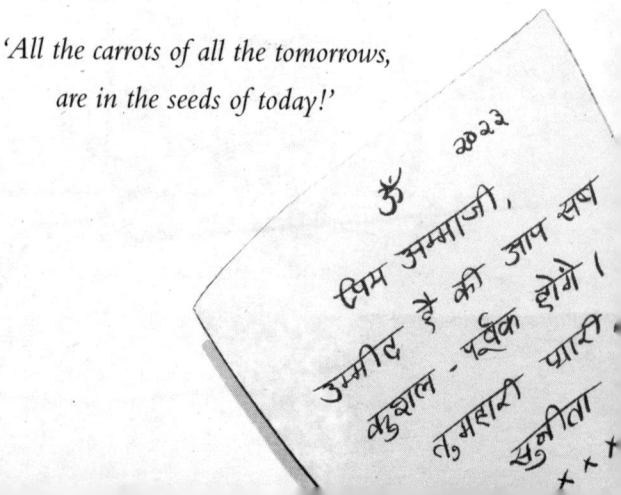

*'All the carrots of all the tomorrows,
are in the seeds of today!'*

ACKNOWLEDGEMENTS

To all the children who read my books, thank you for making my dreams come true!

Special thanks to – Aaria, 梓淇 Annabelle Chi Kei, Akira, Ārya, Eva, 梓浩 Harrison Chi Ho, London, Mischa, Nova, Samuel, Sophia.

Thank you Beverly for starting our journey into children's books together. To Lucy and the children of Harmony House India – thank you for supporting my very first books. Together We Can Change The World.

To my very own 'dragon' teachers, your glowing passion for what you do, shines on. Thank you for teaching me to follow my dreams and not the dreams of others.

To Lucy at Peters, Fraser and Dunlop, and to Eishar, Aimée, Sophie, George, Anita, Sabina, Sam and Ella, my Knights Of family – I couldn't and wouldn't do it without you.

Last but not least – thank you to everyone in cricket, for inspiring my love of this!

JOIN MAYA AND MIND ON ANOTHER ADVENTURE!

A GREAT MYSTERY NEEDS AN EVEN GREATER TEAM ...

MIND and ME

OUT NOW!

SUNITA CHAWDHARY

SUNITA CHAWDHARY
AUTHOR & ILLUSTRATOR

Sunita Chawdhary is a British-Indian author–illustrator, doctor, and mum of two, based in Yorkshire. She studied art and design at Central Saint Martins. Sunita draws on her experience of growing up in Asia, America and Europe to create vibrant, multicultural worlds filled with diverse characters and stories. She believes that children of all cultures and backgrounds should see themselves represented in print. Sunita was commended for the Faber Andlyn BAME (FAB) prize in 2019. She has illustrated the Together We Can Change the World series of picture books, focusing on love and community in all corners of the world. The first title, *Pedro the Puerto Rican Parrot*, was published by Little Steps in April 2021.

KO
KNIGHTS OF

KNIGHTS OF is a multi award-winning inclusive publisher focused on bringing underrepresented voices to the forefront of commercial children's publishing. With a team led by women of colour, and an unwavering focus on their intended readership for each book, Knights Of works to engage with gatekeepers across the industry, including booksellers, teachers and librarians, and supports non-traditional community spaces with events, outreach, marketing and partnerships.